Aphantasia

Experiences, Perceptions, and Insights

Alan Kendle

DARK RIVER

An imprint of Bennion Kearny Ltd.

Published by Dark River, Bennion Kearny Limited
6 Woodside
Churnet View Road
Oakamoor
Staffordshire
ST10 3AE

www.BennionKearny.com

Table of Contents

Preface

This book is about *Aphantasia*; the name people are now using for a condition that affects the ability to view images in your mind's eye. Although I am only recently aware of this condition, it has potentially had the biggest impact on my life.

In this age of awareness, and our desire to understand many things – such as who we are – it does seem extraordinary that such a condition has remained unknown and potentially hidden from me for so long, and not really recognized or explained. How is it not known about in the same way that conditions such as ADHD, Dyslexia, and Autism have become familiar and known to the general public?

This book is my attempt to explore and share how my life, and the lives of others, has been affected by Aphantasia.

Aphantasia is a spectrum disorder because people appear to have differences in how they are affected. Hopefully, reading this book will explain how those variations can manifest and give so many different outcomes.

Many people are likely to live with Aphantasia and never know because the symptoms will not be significant enough to alert them to think more about it. Because it is personal and only seen by them, there is no way to compare. You only look for things like this if you get clues and the nudge to start looking.

I am writing this book to share what I have learned and to try to help others like me to understand this condition better.

I will take a look back into my past to review how I may have been affected as I have grown up. I wish my mum and dad were still alive and I could explain all this to them; it would make so much sense to them as they saw me grow up, struggling and getting stressed with school, learning, and education generally. The words in this book would provide answers, thoughts, and probably lots of questions! They would explain things I never understood at the time, when I could not understand school work and learn in the way others could, as I struggled with reading, spelling, and expression in the written and spoken word.

I want to express my thanks to those scientists, researchers, and other people who have found that Aphantasia exists and provided the understanding for people like me to realize why and how I am affected. It's difficult to put into words but knowing that I am able to help myself more – simply because I understand more – is everything to me.

I need to mention a few people in my world who have helped,

Vanessa – you told me what this is. And helped so much ☺

Caron – the first person to realize I could be more than I thought

My stepchildren – thank you for listening to me when I make no sense

Family – you always said I was different

Friends – just thanks, you might understand me now

Amanda, Sarah, and Christine - ☺ yep I managed to finish this thing, thanks for listening to my ramblings

People at work – you initially must have thought I was mad but never told me, for that support you have my thanks

Alan

About this Book

A number of individuals with Aphantasia have very kindly and generously contributed to this book, offering – as per the subtitle – their experiences, perceptions, and insights into the condition. Contributors' responses are presented alongside their initials, except where anonymity has been requested. In turn, contributors hail from all parts of the world and – in an effort to keep things consistent across the book for a global audience – alternative spelling variants have occasionally been used in place of the original word(s). Furthermore, some responses have been shortened and edited for space and readability reasons.

This book is for both Aphants and non-Aphants and therefore treads a fine line in trying to explain the condition to readers who know little about the condition, whilst expanding and exploring elements for people who know far more about it. Hopefully, readers will find the mix to be a success.

The book does not seek to characterize a typical Aphant. As a spectrum condition, it may not even be possible to do so as people experience their own inimitable versions of the condition. However, some common themes have emerged from the surveys completed, so the book aims to offer a number of more popular perspectives formed around *Alan's journey* of understanding his condition (plus a few of the more unusual!). There will be responses that Aphants will recognize as relatively typical of people with the condition, and others which are more exclusive.

The survey illustrates how Aphantasia is a condition that has rarely held people back. Contributors commonly report how they have achieved personal and professional success, accomplished academic triumphs, delivered wide-ranging and imaginative creative endeavours, and much more, across their lives. As the book will show, very few people consider themselves to be sufferers or that Aphantasia is some form of impediment to goals and attainment. Aphantasia just prompts people to tackle the world in different ways.

A big thank you to everyone who contributed to this book. It would not be the book it is, without you.

Foreword

Three years ago I sat in a London café with an old University friend over a cup of tea. I had asked him to help me coin a term to describe a novel phenomenon, the lifelong lack of the mind's eye. David's classical background transported us from modern Bloomsbury to ancient Athens, where Aristotle had termed the mind's eye 'phantasia'. Its lack, we decided, should, therefore, be christened 'a-phantasia', the 'a-' denoting absence. A slim paper introducing this term (*Lives without imagery: congenital aphantasia*: *Cortex* 2015; 73:378-380) described 21 people who had never visualised. It attracted an unexpected amount of publicity, with notable coverage by Carl Zimmer in the New York Times, James Gallagher on the BBC and the entrepreneur, Blake Ross, on Facebook; two years on, over 11,000 people have been in touch with us, around 3,000 have completed our detailed questionnaires, and we are analysing the flood of resulting data under the auspices of *The Eye's Mind Project*.
(http://medicine.exeter.ac.uk/research/neuroscience/theeyesmind/).

The term 'aphantasia' definitely came into being over those cups of Darjeeling, but was the phenomenon really new to science? Not, in fact, strictly new, but certainly strangely neglected. Dr. Michaela Dewar, co-author of our 2015 paper, pointed me to the previous work of Sir Francis Galton, who devised the first questionnaire probing the vividness of visual imagery in the late nineteenth century. Using his 'breakfast table questionnaire', which invites you to score the 'illumination, definition and colouring' of your recollected image of your 'breakfast table as you sat down to it this morning', Galton recognised that the vividness of imagery was extremely variable. A small handful of those he surveyed claimed to have 'no power of visualising'. But although visual imagery, in general, had received its fair share of scientific attention during the 20ᵗʰ century, the existence of people who lacked this ability entirely was oddly unacknowledged. There was one honourable exception: an American psychologist, Bill Faw, himself a lifelong 'wakeful non-imager', had administered a vividness questionnaire to around 2,500 people, estimating that 2-3% may lack a mind's eye. This work apart, aphantasia had been a blind spot in the eye of imagery science – and this hurt! Many of our contacts describe paying regular visits to the web to see whether anyone was studying this under-researched quirk of their psychology; the arrival of 'aphantasia' opened a door to further dialogue and exploration.

The resulting conversation – to which this book bears witness – has been lively, revealing and compelling. It could not have happened without the internet which allows news to spread and information to be harvested so rapidly. Rarely has research been 'co-constructed' so thoroughly by scientists and participants. There was, it turned out, already a wealth of first-hand knowledge of aphantasia to tap into, with intense interest both from people with aphantasia, whose mental lives are markedly affected by it, and from typical 'visualisers' who are fascinated by the diversity of human experience. The underlying explanation for this degree of interest is, I think, that 'representation in absence' is such a fundamental human capacity; as Robin Dunbar has written 'what sets us apart is a life in the mind, the ability to imagine'. People with aphantasia *can* imagine, sometimes magnificently, but they do so differently, and that difference intrigues us.

There is, of course, a risk in gathering data via the web from interested participants on the back of a news story. There are plenty of opportunities for theory to 'contaminate' data: if I have read that my aphantasia should make it hard – for example – to remember my childhood, my judgment of my memory might well be influenced. And there is a natural tendency, once we have discovered one unusual feature of our make-up, to attribute others to the same cause: 'my mind's eye is dark – so *that's* why I can't learn French!' But these potential pitfalls shouldn't prevent us from listening to, and learning from, the fascinating stories that people with aphantasia have to tell, richly represented in this book.

Although the final analysis is pending, some associations and dissociations with aphantasia look likely to hold true. Here are a few examples. Many people with aphantasia – though by no means all – describe greater than average difficulty in recognising faces, finding it hard, for instance, to pick out a single actress through changes of hairstyle and costume. Why this should be is unclear, but the association is intriguing. Many, though not all, describe a factual style of autobiographical memory, 're-inhabiting' the past less vividly than most of us. Many, as evocatively described in the pages of this book, describe themselves as more 'present' and less prone to emotions like longing or lingering disgust than their more visually-imaginative friends. In general, the gains and losses from aphantasia are finely balanced: I think of it as a variation in experience rather than a disorder or a medical 'condition'.

What of the *dissociations*? These were already on show in our small original sample of 21 people. The majority of people with aphantasia experience visual imagery during dreams, though not during ordinary wakefulness, suggesting an important distinction between sleeping and waking, or involuntary and voluntary, imagery. The majority, by a slim margin, experience imagery in other modalities, most often auditory: so the mind's ear need not be deaf because the mind's eye is blind, although it certainly is so in some, including Alan.

Is aphantasia, then, one thing or many? And what kind of a thing is it – a quirk, a symptom, a syndrome? Resolving these questions requires more research, but it won't surprise me at all if it turns out to be complex. We know that visualising involves a wide network of areas in the brain, involved, among other things, in decision making, attention, memory, and vision; it would be surprising if such a complex function could not be disturbed in more than one way.

So, some hard work needs to be done to 'triangulate' between i) the fascinating first-person evidence presented in this book, ii) measurement of relevant abilities using robust psychological tests in people with varying levels of imagery vividness and iii) brain scanning to look for corresponding differences in brain structure and function. Although studies of this general kind have been underway for many years, the recognition of imagery extremes – aphantasia and its counterpart, hyperphantasia – has opened a new and exciting avenue for enquiry. Work in my lab and others is travelling down it.

This book provides a treasure trove of observations and insights for anyone interested in imagery in general and aphantasia in particular. There may still be science to do before we can draw firm conclusions about the significance of extreme imagery but there is poetry in the subject that we can enjoy in the meantime. Here, for example, are the beautiful words of the aphantasic JK, from Chapter 2, describing his or her widespread lack of imagery:

'I can't recall smells at all, but I can recall words for them. I know that lilac is a "soft" scent that makes my toes tingle; it reminds me of my mother and summer mountain sunshine.'

And here, ML, in Chapter 7, describing what it is like to remember an event in the absence of imagery, with the precision of a haiku:

'It is a story. A quick-fire retelling. A mental diary.'

The deepest lesson from aphantasia surely concerns human diversity. We all tend to regard our own experience as normal; inevitably, it supplies our standard for comparison. It is easy, therefore, to fail to recognise quite startling differences between our inner lives. Revealing them is interesting, explanatory and sometimes liberating. The final words of Alan's book, a quotation from L, are well chosen:

'I live in the now. I cannot live in the past. I cannot dream of the future. I have had many very spiritual experiences before I even knew that I was different than most people. I have done things differently, and that is OK with me.'

Professor Adam Zeman, Professor of Cognitive and Behavioural Neurology, University of Exeter

Chapter 1: What is Aphantasia?

The ability of the human mind to conjure up an image – on demand – is taken for granted by many people. Typically, if someone is asked to picture a clifftop, an orange square, a toaster, or another common object or scene, in their mind, the majority are able to do so fairly effortlessly.

People with Aphantasia, on the other hand, cannot picture these objects or scenes. They lack the ability to generate particular imagery within their 'mind's eye' through conscious effort. Paradoxically, visual imagery often appears when in a sub-conscious state such as sleep.

Although some clinical tests have been devised to diagnose Aphantasia, in essence an individual will know if they have Aphantasia when "Can you visualize images in your mind?" *fails* to ring true.

Aphantasia is a spectrum condition which affects people to different degrees along a range of linked symptoms. These linked symptoms vary in terms of scope and severity, so one key point is that the experiences of Aphants can vary quite significantly between individuals.

Whilst the inability to visualize imagery is the defining characteristic of Aphantasia, additional elements commonly reported can include the inability to recall music, and the inability to recall a smell or a feeling. A significant number of Aphants also believe they have a condition called prosopagnosia: difficulty in recognizing people's faces (also known as 'face blindness'). Another concept that some Aphants commonly recount is the inability to sense a 'feeling' in response to a picture or word, for example, feeling shivery if someone mentions that there was a spider in their shoe and they placed their foot into it.

History

Although the concept of Aphantasia appears to date back to the psychologist Sir Francis Galton in the 1880s, it remained a relatively unexplored condition for more than a century. Indeed, the term Aphantasia was only coined in 2015, by Professor Adam Zeman and his colleagues at the University of Exeter in the United Kingdom. Zeman and his team are leading the way in researching and better understanding the condition.

In the 1880s, Galton did very well in describing the phenomenon now known as Aphantasia in his paper *Statistics of Mental Imagery*. He had realized that people visualize things to different degrees and set about to explain to what extent. In particular, he asked his colleagues to describe their breakfast tables. Through doing so, he discovered that, whilst some individuals would describe the scene so vividly that Galton himself could almost picture it, others used minimal descriptions, and some were unable to do so at all. As a side note, Galton invited Charles Darwin (a cousin) to participate, and Darwin was found to have a very well-developed ability to visualize; he described his breakfast table scene in great detail.

Galton carried out some further research and even went so far as to determine that, "The missing faculty seems to be replaced so serviceably by other modes of conception... Men who declare themselves entirely deficient in the power of seeing mental pictures can nevertheless give life-like descriptions of what they have seen."

What causes Aphantasia?

The cause of the condition is not yet known. Most people with the condition are born with it, though there has been one documented case of a man who developed Aphantasia following minor surgery (he was in his 60s at the time).

The main reason the cause is not known is because the process and mechanisms of visualization, within the human brain, is not fully understood. Although there are theories based in philosophy, psychology, and neuroscience, it is the evidence in neuroscience that is the most convincing with credible explanations surrounding the idea that the brain can call upon past experiences and memories – through neuronal firing and activity across a number of brain regions including the frontal, parietal, temporal, and occipital lobes – to generate imagery. The occipital lobe is part of the cerebral cortex and responsible for visual processing, whilst the frontal and parietal lobes help to organize visualization. An Aphant's inability to visualize is likely to come from a functional change somewhere in the linked system.

Although people with Aphantasia cannot consciously produce images, they find other ways to remember and describe their experiences. In turn, the ability to visualize consciously is not the same as dreaming. Many Aphants report being able to dream whilst asleep with vivid images and scenes, and even custom content. Therefore, Aphantasia appears to be a lack of voluntary imagery. Some, however, report that they do not dream visually, and will only recall dreams by text, narrative, or plot points.

People with Aphantasia do, however, possess a visual memory although they use facts to recognize objects, places, and people. They may, for example, remember that the girl in their lecture class who is quiet has striking blue eyes, or that the cousin they met at a wedding has a chiselled face and shoulder-length brown hair. The world of a person with the condition is based more upon description than imagery.

Prevalence

Aphantasia is thought to affect between two and three percent of the population. This figure is an estimate and it must be recognized that the condition and its boundaries are still being identified.

Commonly, people with the condition may not know they have the condition at all, or come to realize later in life. If a person has had the condition since birth or very early childhood, then it is normal for them not to be able to visualize without realizing it is something that others are able to do.

Impact

There seems to be, on the whole, few if any limitations in life for people with Aphantasia. It has not been recorded to link significantly with distress, discomfort, or cognitive or functional deficits in individuals. However, some individuals report feeling sadness at their lack of ability to recall the faces or visual memories of loved ones that have passed away, or their ability to visualize past, meaningful experiences. Many people with Aphantasia would describe their memory as 'poor' but have a great capacity for remembering facts.

Whilst most people, when imagining, will use visualization and allow their mind to produce detailed and vivid images, Aphants will use language to bring something to life. As a result, some Aphants have become writers of fiction, using their highly developed language skills to produce absorbing literature. On the flip side, others with Aphantasia will often report that they struggle to read descriptive fiction – for example, the long prose describing countryside or a cityscape – as it is almost meaningless to them; they may find themselves reading the text several times over to grasp what the author is trying to convey.

So, without further ado, let us start to explore this most fascinating of human conditions in more detail.

*

[Alan Kendle] So I am 55-years-old and have lived my life without knowing (until recently) that others encounter the world and their mental experiences differently. Honestly, I thought everyone saw and heard the same way as me in their mind. I had no reason to think otherwise.

From my encounters, Aphantasia appears to have differences in almost every person with the condition that I have spoken with, or written to. I am starting to think that we could all have unique mental standpoints and everyone will be different in some way.

Do I consider myself a *sufferer*? I am not sure if I am. But I am certainly profoundly affected. The word sufferer has negative connotations, and I would like a better word than sufferer. It is not a word that fits the effects of the condition, and does not describe how I really feel about having it. Nearly every person with Aphantasia to whom I have mentioned this theory of being a *sufferer* has also disagreed with that wording. Some quite strongly.

There are what I see as contradictions with the condition. Firstly, I have a vivid imagination! (Although I can never see the things I can imagine in my mind.) I cannot even visualize family or friends that I have lost, or those still alive. Instead, my imagination takes the form of playing with concepts and ideas, working out how things could fit together. As an example, I like to think how something like "six degrees of separation" could impact on social networks in the future. These thoughts come together like a puzzle hanging in free space that I try and slot together. They do not happen with any structural form in my mind, just ideas with no arrangement.

I should also say, at this point, that images and visualizations are not the only thing missing from my mind's eye. With music, I hear no songs, sounds, or any other audio in my mind other than the content heard from the real world outside my head in real time.

I was totally surprised to learn that a friend could not only visualize people she knows but could hear them talking as well (and in their own voice, the voice that person usually speaks in). I can hear myself speak, obviously, in my voice that the world hears – I just don't have an inner voice that speaks to me or which I can listen to talking. When I think of something, there is no voice; it just is the imagination of the words being said – just the essence of it. There is no structure or form but it is still a recognizable thing mentally, it's not a feeling but more like a presence. It's like when you catch sight of something in the corner of your peripheral version; you are aware it's there but without the detail of seeing it right in front of you.

I found out that I had Aphantasia, in 2016, when my wife heard a discussion on the subject on the radio. The radio guest was explaining what they could and couldn't do with their 'mind's eye'. When she came home from work, my wife said, "You have to look this up and listen. Because this is you!"

Even though my wife did not entirely appreciate the condition being discussed, it was enough for her to realize how it might relate to me from the descriptions made, and explanations given. Straightaway I wanted to know more about this term 'Aphantasia'. Why is so little known? I had never heard of it before, ever.

I downloaded the radio show and the rest is history.

So now I realize I don't have a mind's eye; it's kind of funny, but once you realize something significant about your life, you get a new sense of perspective and understanding. It's like if someone says there are a lot of yellow cars on the road today. You start to look for them when, before that moment, you never gave it a second thought. In my case, I am constantly looking for something that is *not* there (visual imagery) but once that seed is sown, it is difficult not to.

As I go about my daily business, I know my brain must be able to store images in some way because I can recognize things. I look at a car and know it is a car, including its make and model. In turn, I remember the names of people I know.

I can imagine and mentally recall things, but rather than a picture or video imagery in my mind, it is the essence of an image. It is the abstract nature or character of the thing I recall. No feelings or emotions are associated with this recall. I have struggled to understand this, let alone explain it.

If I think of my house, or buildings, or even cars – size seems to be a constraining factor, my mind limits the area/size that I can mentally focus on in my mind. If I try to think of large things, or try and mentally move back to get a better view (like a city landscape) I only seem to get the impression of a small bit of the horizon rather than the whole thing. It feels to be self-limiting with me unable to move my focus or mental gaze across the horizon in real time.

I can remember things but not to any level of detail. I can't remember my parents' faces. If I try and imagine them, I get the essence of what I am thinking about but there's no real detail; not enough to know who it is. It's only a slight mental image that fades away as I try to concentrate on it, like a cloud on a windy day. It's almost like the detail of mental imagery is inversely proportional to the mental focus used to access it.

That's probably the toughest part the condition; not remembering people who are no longer with you or anyone close.

As mentioned, I have no inner voice. I can say words in my mind but they have no form or physical substance. I hear no music, voices or anything created by my mind in my mind. I was surprised when a colleague told me about their own inner voice.

I am not able to recall smells or sensations of touch. I have the five senses and can smell, touch, etc., but I cannot store that sensory event to recall at a later date. Having said that, I know I can recall and remember some senses given the right circumstances and the correct trigger, but I do not know what they or it is.

When I close my eyelids, I see no visual imagery. I have always thought this is what everyone sees; I guess I never questioned it before and thought when people described mental visual images, they were just being expressive and not reporting on real life. When my eyes lids are closed, it's just blackness; there is nothing else I can see.

*

Alan realized he had Aphantasia in 2016, and a great many contributors to this book have, likewise, only come to identify their condition within the last few years as Aphantasia's public profile has grown. This means that people have formally recognized their Aphantasia at various ages, from teenage years to more senior stages in life.

People have picked up that they were Aphants following conversations with friends, family, and colleagues; others from newspaper articles and online sources including the BBC website, Reddit, and Facebook.

[DG] I was doing a course on method acting (Strasberg Method) – when our mentor suggested a scenario and that we should picture it. I realized that everyone could – EXCEPT me.

[ML] At school, we were told to imagine a tree and draw it. As the best artist in the class I was upset to see everyone else making a fair attempt at this, but when I closed my eyes I saw nothing. I spent the next week memorizing a tree structure to make sure that it didn't happen again, but it is still just a stylised drawing. I can only draw (quite well) from life really.

[AS] I saw a headline of a New York Times article on Facebook. I think it was something like, "Picture this. Some people just can't." And I thought, "Hmm... that sounds like me."

And I clicked on it and read it.

It completely floored me. I had no idea most people could literally picture things. Like, see an actual picture. I always thought it was more of a metaphorical thing. So, I asked my husband to read the article and asked if he could picture an actual picture in his mind. And he said he could and was really surprised when I told him I couldn't.

[L] My husband and I were out to dinner for our 18th anniversary. Sitting across from each other at a table for two, we were having a discussion. During this discussion, visualization was brought up. I said I could not visualize... can you?

"Of course, I can," he said. "I can visualize you in my mind."

I was confused and asked him how he could do that?

He went on to say, "I can superimpose your Mom's face on you."

This is the point where I was really shocked!

"What?! That's not normal."

We had a lively debate about who was normal. Him, a very capable visualizer or me, non-visualizer.

I thought I was normal and he was exceptional with his ability. I thought being human was being shut off from "the other side" that I strongly believe exists.

We decided to ask people we know, take personal surveys; if they could visualize so we could compare our findings and continue the discussion...

I found out I was the oddball. Everyone I talked to could visualize!

I would ask "Can you visualize?" Them, closing their eyes, "Yeah, what do you want me to visualize?"

[TM] I was studying to be a teacher in college. We were talking about having kids visualize to help figure out spelling a word. Forever, I had heard people say, "Picture in your head…" I just thought that people were talking metaphorically. It was only in that class discussion in college that I realized that people actually really do see pictures, words, and so forth. I was stunned.

[Anonymous] I read Blake Ross's Facebook post, after seeing a friend share it with her husband (who also has Aphantasia). It was less about realizing I had Aphantasia, and more about realizing (and confirming) that everyone else could actually see things in their minds.

[AT] I was listening to a podcast! It's called Stuff You Should Know, and they did a whole episode on Aphantasia. They began the show with a guided imagery script about imagining a beach and the sea, and so on, and I was thinking 'man this is pointless…' Until they 'revealed' that most people actually see and hear and feel the situation described to them! I was so surprised. Like a lot of Aphants, I didn't realize I was unusual. I'd always just assumed that 'picture a scene' was a figure of speech.

[BM] A friend with Aphantasia posted an article on Facebook. That led to discussions among our friends, and it made me realize that a "mind's eye" is not simply a metaphor used by most people. I always assumed that a "mind's eye", "mind's ear", "mind's nose", "mind's tongue", etc. were convenient ways of describing more abstract experiences common to all people. I never thought that some people actually saw things, heard things, smelled things, tasted things, etc. in their minds. I have almost no conscious mental sensory experiences at all, but I have quite an active and detailed inner world despite that fact. So, I always thought I was like everyone else.

[JA] I have depression and anxiety and was having a rough few years. Long story short, my mom has – from as early as I can remember – told me to close my eyes and imagine... as a kid, I would try but didn't understand the concept or what I was supposed to 'see'.

So, fast forward to 33-years-old and I'm visiting with my mom and I'm stressed out and she again tells me to close my eyes and visualize myself somewhere peaceful like the 'ocean'.

I agree, close my eyes and listen to her words.

She's saying things like, "Now picture the sand, the colour of the water."

I remember feeling frustrated with her words "picture" and "visualize"; after a while I open my eyes and I'm agitated so I ask, "What do you mean "picture"? I don't see anything."

I remember the look on her face. It was a mixture of confusion and shock. She asked me questions like, "You can't see the ocean? The colour of the water? Hear the waves?"

I said no, and thought, how crazy to see things that aren't here right now... but it bothered me... so I later started googling things like, "Do some people really see images in their mind?"

The thought seemed absurd and I thought my mom was unusual. I then saw the word Aphantasia and began googling it and reading about it. I was shocked; I had no idea that me seeing complete darkness when I closed my eyes and tried to see things was not the norm for everyone.

[CS2] I was listening to a podcast on Aphantasia; they described the condition, and it didn't really click at that point.

I've always understood "visualizing" as a more abstract concept, and thought that was the case for everybody. The hosts of the podcast asked the listeners to close their eyes and try to visualize a beach (good thing I wasn't driving at the time).

So I did.

I didn't see anything (maybe a faint flash of a shoreline for a fraction of a second, then that was gone), but I had the idea of a beach in my head. The hosts went on to describe the extent of the details they could each "see" in their minds' eyes, including colour and movement. My mind was blown! You mean people actually see things when they visualize?!? That's amazing! I was (and still am) fascinated with that idea.

[JS] I was sat at home in the sitting room on my laptop with the rest of my family around me watching TV. I came across the BBC article "Aphantasia: A life without mental images" and after reading it, I sat there dumbstruck. I asked my family if they could actually imagine things like images or memories in their heads and they could. I just couldn't believe it and still can't to some extent.

[AS2] I discovered, through a book club, that I read books as words rather than visualize the book as a 'film/movie' in my head. I was aware though that I had difficulties recognizing people, unless I knew them extremely well and saw them often. I was also aware that when asked to visualize something as part of a Dyslexia training session I was doing, I simply couldn't. Everyone else in the room could, and so I just went with the flow and never said anything.

[JT] Guided imagery meditation. I was unable to "see", but others in the group would describe visualization as though they were picturing things (because they were!).

[KB] I was 36 when I became aware of the term Aphantasia and the percentage of people who couldn't visualize in their minds' eyes. I am a yoga teacher and knew that people could visualize in guided meditation. However, I always thought it was a minority that could visualize and a skill to be learned and mastered, not a norm.

[MC] I read a book about a girl with synaesthesia ("A Mango-Shaped Space" by Wendy Mass). While I had heard of that condition before, based on my experience of the world, I assumed that when someone "saw" letters and numbers as colours, they were seeing it in the real world somehow. In the book, the girl "sees" smells and sounds as colour, at which point I realized she was experiencing the synaesthesia in her mind.

[MR2] I have always had difficulty visualizing. I've attempted group-guided hypnosis and meditations, but seemed to be the only person in the room that had difficulty. I had always attributed it to not having enough practice and that it would get easier if I worked on it more.

[RH] I was working an extremely long shift, a bit more than 17 hours of physical and mental demand. I had less than my normal amount of sleep the night prior. I was close to finishing and was extremely tired.

All of a sudden, I started thinking in visuals. Completely visual. It was like controlling a movie in my head. I could "think" so amazingly quickly, in only visuals. I thought that I was hallucinating.

When describing to a very close co-worker, he said, I always think in images. I was shocked. Unfortunately, after sleeping, I was not able to "see" mental images any longer. Occasionally, I will get a flash of colour or a quick "still" image when very relaxed, but I cannot control it. I cannot force it.

[MR] I was berating my husband for counting kangaroos in the paddock instead of keeping his eyes on the road while driving. He told me he took a mental picture of it then counted them in the picture. I thought he was joking and he thought he must have a special power, but then we discovered that everyone else could do it – just not me. Later, he saw a story about Aphantasia and we realized it was describing my experiences to a T.

*

The label 'sufferer' is one that sits uneasily with many Aphants. To some it is pejorative, to others a term that fails to characterize the condition at all accurately.

[MB] I can't think of a better word.

[AK] No, I don't think of myself as a sufferer! I am an Aphant, I have Aphantasia… if one considers it a condition. To me it is the normal state, I know no different.

[JT] No, I don't "suffer" from Aphantasia. My brain works differently.

[Anonymous] No – I think it's just a variation of the human condition. I feel there are upsides and downsides to whatever brain configuration you have, and I'm sure there are lots of other variations we don't notice. I would describe myself as 'having Aphantasia' or as someone 'with Aphantasia', or maybe an 'Aphant' colloquially.

[MU] Yes, I am a sufferer. The condition has definitely affected me my whole life in a negative way.

[AS] I don't know that I would call it suffering. It's not a physical pain, but it is very upsetting to find out about at first. And I'm sad that I can't picture things now that I know about it.

[AT] I don't like the word 'sufferer' because I'm not really suffering. Parts of my life do suffer because of Aphantasia though. I am hopeless at remembering people, or putting names to faces, not amazing with directions, and have no chance of telling you what I ate for dinner last night.

I do love the word neurodivergent! It sounds so sci-fi, but really is just a practical way to label these quirks that aren't a bad thing.

[BM] No, I am not a 'sufferer' because of the lack of a mind's eye, mind's ear, etc. I am simply a member of a minority group that experiences the connection between thought and conscious mental sensory experiences in a slightly different way. I would describe myself as 'normal'.

[CW] I do not suffer. I am just not neurotypical.

[PA] No. I am a realist. Other people are tricked to believe that they can "see" things with their eyes closed.

[CS] I never used to. It was normal to me until I discovered it was abnormal. I still wouldn't say I suffer with it, I get on just fine. I think you can only suffer from something if you develop it. You are either born blind, which is normal for that person; or it is developed later on, and that person would suffer from blindness. I guess I just have it, I do not suffer.

[ML] Not sufferer; I would go with disadvantaged – as in 'partially blind'.

[DS] I call Aphantasia a condition that I have, but I don't suffer from it. I look at it more as my style of thinking. Most other people have a visualization style.

[GD] Just another variety of being human.

[JK2] I have Aphantasia, I don't suffer from Aphantasia. I don't feel pain, distress, loss, injury, or harm simply because I don't have a visual imagination. I also don't feel that I am at a real disadvantage.

People who are "suffering" are pretty aware of it, while I went through 35 years of life blissfully unaware that others had a totally different imaginative experience.

[JL] Bearer? Possessor?

[L] I refer to it as "my blackness."

[JR] I say that I have a condition or a syndrome. To me, suffering implies physical and/or emotional pain. And I'm not suffering in any way. Struggling at times, but not suffering.

[MB2] I don't consider myself a sufferer. "Afflicted" would be a better word. Aphantasia has not caused me any significant pain in my life so far.

[MR] I 'HAVE Aphantasia', but don't 'suffer' from it. Perhaps experience would be a better word.

[PW] Not at all, just different.

[SC] No, it doesn't really cause any suffering. I suffer from Amnesia, but I just have Aphantasia, just like if I had red hair, I wouldn't suffer from red hair. I would just have red hair.

[TS] I definitely suffer from Aphantasia.

[ST] I am not a sufferer I just consider myself someone who doesn't do pictures.

[KB] No. I have never suffered. I have always been academically advanced and have a successful life. I have never thought of it as a problem or disadvantage. Yes, my mind works a bit differently, and that is okay. Like everything, it has pros and cons. I am content with how I am. It doesn't hinder my life in any way.

[CS2] I like the old joke: "Do you suffer from a mental illness?" – "No, I enjoy it!"

*

For many non-Aphants/Visualizers, the most intriguing initial question is what does an Aphant actually 'see' when closing their eyes?

[AR] Nothing.

[DS] Blackness.

[AY] Nothing.

[MC] I see blackness.

[AT] Absolutely nothing! It is literally just darkness. No light, no sight!

[CS] Absolutely nothing, there is just black. I tried for ages when I first found out that I was missing something, it just gave me a headache.

[JC] Black nothingness.

[CH] Black. Do visualizers see mental images better when they close their eyes? I've always wondered why we get this question.

[CS2] Just absolute blackness. If I try really hard, mostly at night it may be easier, I can see grey shadow-like shapes of things for fractions of a second, then they're gone.

[JS] Blackness. All I'm looking at is the back of my eyelids.

[JK] Black, the insides of my eyelids.

[CW] Darkness, occasional phosphenes.

[JK2] Darkness. The back of my eyelids. Sometimes there might be very faint, paisley-like designs in blues, greens, and greys floating around in there. It gets slightly stronger if I'm in total darkness.

[JL] "Void" (I can say black, but it's not black, it's just... nothingness).

[JR] Generally, just grey but if there's a lot of light or I'm in sunshine, the colour is considerably lighter, like a light yellow or beige as the light is going through my eyelids. A while back I noticed that when I was in pain, the dentist was drilling a tooth, I saw orange, red and green flashes that remained for a few seconds or longer, depending on how long the pain continued. These colours were irregularly shaped, sort of like a star with many points. Jagged stars would be an apt description.

[MR2] I don't see anything. Just a lot of blackness.

[LH] I see darkness, no images but quite often it's like looking at something under a microscope – lots of tiny moving floaters. I don't know if that is just the back of my eyelids or floaters on my eyes.

[ND] Blackness, sometimes light coming through my eyelids.

[SR] Different shades of black, depending on the lighting.

[TM] I only see darkness when I close my eyes. No colours or images appear.

[MH] Billions of fine whitish pin-tipped pointed dots set against an entirely black background.

[MU] I see nothing. I also hear, taste, experience, nothing internally.

[RH] Nothing, the backs of my eyelids!

[PA] I see the back of my eyelids. It is black.

[PW] Nothing, just blackness or 'fuzz'.

[RW] It's dark with some very faint random bits of light. I've always assumed that bits of light are due to an imperfect eyelid seal, even though I get them even in pitch dark rooms.

[SB] I get a headache if I try long enough. But I don't actually "see" anything.

[TS] Black. There's the black background and the multicolour interference pattern that's probably the afterimage from seeing light. Or whatever it is. It sometimes resembles shapes.

[VD] Blackness with varying darkness based on ambient light.

*

For non-Aphants, understanding how people with Aphantasia can conceptualize physical objects without using visual imagery can be difficult to process. So, what happens when Aphants are asked to visualize something, something such as their house...

[RH] I can't really describe what happens. I can describe my home to you. I can tell you the style, the materials, the colours. I can describe the layout, but I can't "see" any of this in my mind. While I am not particularly good at drawing, I often draw things to help explain visual things to others.

[JK2] I can describe facts about my house: it's a West-facing, two-storey, cookie-cutter, stucco thing with vague Spanish influence. It's beige with green shutters. Two garages – a two car to the right, facing North, and a single car garage facing West.

I don't "see" it in my head or anything, but that's what it looks like. I could trace its invisible outline with an invisible hand if I needed to find a way to describe an angle or slope or something, but I still don't see anything.

[AT] I can tell you exactly what the house is like! But I can't bring the image of it to mind, nor can I smell it, or… imagine the sounds.

It's more like I have a paragraph to 'read' (not that I see the words), and it describes the environment of my house.

Maybe it's like trying to imagine the Parthenon in its glory without any photographic records to base it on. You could read from Wikipedia ("The Parthenon is a peripteral octastyle Doric temple with Ionic architectural features. It stands on a platform or stylobate of three steps. In common with other Greek temples, it is of post and lintel construction and is surrounded by columns ("peripteral") carrying an entablature.") but you're never going to actually see it as it was. This is always the hardest bit to try to explain to a neurotypical person!

[TS] The best I can see is a split second flash of what I was trying to visualize, like a dark grey shape against a black background.

I can kinda visualize 3D space though. I can place the 'idea' of the objects I'm visualizing in different mental locations and imagine them moving, running, jumping and so on.

It's like a pitch black theatre where I know the play well enough to somewhat know what each person is doing at each moment. I just can't see them.

[Anonymous] One of my major ways of thinking is what I call 'spatial' – it's hard to describe, but I have a 3D representation of form that's not visible. Echolocation might be a good analogy? Or a computer-generated 3D landscape with no lighting – the landscape is still there and the computer knows where it is, but it's not visible.

When I think of my house, I think of it this way, with some ideas/feelings of colour (non-visual). It's not particularly detailed (though I can zoom in on things to make them more detailed) – think a mid-nineties computer-generated 3D landscape, or slightly-better resolution than Minecraft. I also usually have a north-point in the 'spatial' (I generally keep track of where north is in real life, though I get it wrong sometimes).

[AR] I am unable to visualize anything. However, sometimes I am able to get a brief glimpse. Usually, I recall a list of facts about whatever it is I am trying to visualize.

[LH] There is absolutely no image. I close my eyes really tightly because I think maybe if I don't allow other sources of imagery to enter my brain then I may have more chance of visualizing. It never works. I live in hope.

[TM] When I try to visualize something, a narrative starts running in my head. If you say, think of your house then my internal voice will start describing my house. My description will be pretty lengthy and filled with words that would paint a picture for people who can create images in their heads. However, no image appears for me, just the auditory version of my physical world.

[MB2] I can get a split second flash of an image in my mind's eye, but I can't maintain it to look at it in any detail. I hesitate to even call my brief attempted visualizations "images" because they are so incredibly dim and non-vibrant, almost as if dust or a very grainy film effect has been placed over them.

In that split-second, the image gets washed away by some sort of grey wave of dust. If my image was dimly lit to begin with, the wave turns off the lights completely.

When I try and visualize something, it feels as if my mind's eye is an Etch-a-Sketch which is being shaken constantly, making it nearly impossible to visualize a full image, let alone focus on it.

I can visualize John Travolta's chin for a moment, but if I try to visualize his face from there, it's game over – grey wash. If I try again to visualize his face, it's far less detailed than my visualization of his chin, and gone in a split second before I can zone in on the chin.

It's a bit frustrating, admittedly.

[JA] I see nothing; if my eyes are closed it is black with an orange colour depending on lighting. I remember it off of memory… which is hard to explain. I do not see anything at all, I just know (my childhood home for example) was a small one-storey house, in a box shape. No extra decorations or building accessories. It was a light peachy brown colour. Had four bedrooms and a long hallway… but I know this from memory, from information, nothing visual.

[MU] I can see it for about a tenth of a second, then it vanishes.

[Anonymous] If I try to visualize something with my eyes closed I will simply see black – whatever I try. I always explain to other people that my mind works kind of like a robot. I just have a lot of data (in words) stored, that will help me to remember and recognize things. E.g., for my house I know how many m^2 it is, how many rooms it has, and how they are attached to each other, etc. I know the colour of my couch, table, kitchen, bedroom, etc. simply because I have stored this as data in my head and not because I can see it.

[PW] There are only concepts, like geometric shapes, and facts, like colours and sizes.

[MR] I think of words that describe it but do not actually visualize it.

[MC] Well, I never 'try to visualize'. My mind has always been a black void, and for the majority of my life I did not even know that visualization was possible for other people.

When I think of my house, I think of myself in relation to its space. I know how the rooms are arranged, and what it feels like to be in any of them or move between them. I know the items that are in each room, and where they are in the room. It is a combination of spatial awareness and facts.

[DS] When trying to think of an object, I usually have the general shape come to mind. Thinking of my house, it's a rectangle (if I were actually looking at the front of the house). If I think of a person, either the shape of a generic head or body shape. These are not visualized in my head, just the idea of that shape is there.

I've tried to articulate what that 'idea' is before, and it's very difficult. It feels more like a spatial awareness. I have a sense of a face when I think about my father or my wife. Once I have that sense, I can try to think of details of that face. I consider where the nose is and the general shape of that person's nose is now in my spatial awareness, but the sense of the entire face has disappeared. It's one shape at a time.

[BM] I have detailed memories and concepts related to the thing I try to 'visualize'. Those memories and concepts have to do with colour, sound, direction, proportion, orientation, smell, relationships, abstract characteristics, etc. When I try to think about something, such as my house, I activate the relevant concepts and relationships to help me build a coherent understanding of that something. No mental pictures, sounds, etc. are necessary.

Chapter 2: Explaining the Condition to Others

One of the potential challenges for people with Aphantasia is trying to explain the condition to people who are able to visualize. It does not give itself over, easily, to descriptions that visualizers can comprehend quickly. Whilst the concept of 'not being able to see anything' seems clear enough, effective metaphors can prove harder to come by.

In turn, some people express disbelief that such a condition exists because it is alien to how they navigate and experience the world. This can mean that sharing the condition becomes twofold.

1. Convincing someone that it is possible not to have a mind's eye.

2. Getting them to understand exactly what that entails.

*

[Alan] If I close my eyes, I literally see black with no additional imagery. Always. Nothing I try can create any images in my mind. If I try imagining a famous song, or singer singing, or talking – I see nothing, I hear nothing, smell nothing, feel no sense of touch. I only get black and silence; I don't get any words and images.

When I try to explain Aphantasia to people, it takes time to describe the concept; they just don't imagine you cannot see what they can visualize in their own minds. To be honest, why would they think other people could be that different to them?

Although I have known about the condition for the last year or so, I haven't found an easy way to explain it to people when talking about it for the first time. I try to discuss it without them looking at me in a way which translates to "Are you joking?!?"

I want to try and explain the concept of having no mind's eye in very simple terms; as something that makes sense to people. The best way I can describe it is, "Like having no VCR in your head, no way to store or play back images." I have no ability to record and then play back anything that might be available from my visual mental library (memory). For me, the same goes for music. When I have heard music, I can't play it back in my head.

Explaining the condition to someone sceptical can be interesting, so choosing your examples wisely, rather than just trying to stumble into it, pays dividends.

So, how to start? First up (in my view) don't attempt to explain Aphantasia to someone in a few minutes. Often, with a new idea, some dialogue is needed as it involves fresh thinking and understanding from the person you are talking to. Therefore, I think the first thing is to find the opportunity to explain matters slowly, in the time available, to do it justice.

Context is the best way to establish the groundwork for discussing Aphantasia. It's not a subject you can drop into a conversation like something on the television from the evening before. First, find out what the person you are talking to sees in their own mind (in terms of mental images) and then explain what you see. From there, it's a discussion and an exchange of concepts, ideas, and thoughts to converge in a common understanding.

Once people realize that Aphantasia exists, they tend to ask simple questions; possibly just to explore and comprehend their understanding of the condition. Having said all the above, I don't really try and explain Aphantasia to people I have just met, and there are two main reasons for that.

1. One person I explained the condition to realized they were a sufferer as well. They were surprised to say the least but, afterwards, I felt it was better for people to discover Aphantasia for themselves, rather than having someone just tell them.

2. It is not easy to describe the condition effectively, and I normally don't do a great job of explaining it initially. I have found I need to adapt and change depending on the way people follow my usually poor explanation of Aphantasia.

I realize they sound like weak reasons and I should try harder to help others discover more about their own minds and conditions if they have it. But, when people realize that they are different to most others, I think it can feel unsettling.

*

How do contributors explain their Aphantasia to others?

[CW] I don't.

[CS2] "You know when you close your eyes, and you can picture a cat? Yeah, I can't do that."

[CH] I ask them to picture a duck. I ask them what kind of duck. Then I tell them I can't do that.

[TS] Can you think of a red apple and actually see it in your head? I can't. I can't visualize anything in my head. If I try to think of my wife's face, I can't see it. I can't bring up smells, sense or touch or how a dog barking sounds either.

[PW] Not very well actually. :) I just say that I don't see any pictures in my mind, but that clearly isn't really enough to get the point across to most people.

[MC] I describe it thus: think about walking through your house in the middle of the night when all the lights are out.

You roughly know where everything is, because you are very familiar with the space, even if you can't see it. This is my mind and memories — darkness, but awareness of the space I am or was in.

[JK] Tell them to close their eyes and picture something (like a red triangle or the beach) and ask them if they can see the image with colour in their mind, and then tell them I can't do that.

[JK2] It's hard. I used to say it was like being in a dark room or a dark movie set – I know that there's a chair in there and I know its approximate location, what colour it is, and other facts, I just can't see it.

I quickly learned that this doesn't help them understand, because they simply overlay their visual imagination over the dark room!

The best I can do now is say that I just think about the word 'horse' and I have an arsenal of descriptive words at my disposal that I use to describe the concept of 'horse'. I don't have a visual image of a horse, but I know how to use words to describe a horse doing a variety of things. I can describe a horse rearing up in the ocean surf – the details changing depending on the setting, time of day, weather, and the type of horse in question. I simply don't see any of it.

[DS] I mention the "mind's eye" that allows you to see images in your head. Most people immediately understand what I'm talking about. I tell them that my mind's eye is blind and I have no images in my head.

[BM] Ask the person to describe something that is not connected to a single, clear image – e.g., describe what "rich" means, describe what "love" means, describe what the number "ten" means. If they can describe those things to others using words, then those ideas are not dependent on mental images since one person cannot see another person's mental images. Then point out that everyone can use the same method to describe a sunset, a house, a cat, etc. What those of us without a mind's eye do is think about and negotiate our way through the world using descriptions and representations of concepts that are not tied directly to mental images.

[AY] I always tell someone to try picture a loved one's face. Then explain that I cannot do that, and that I have no idea how it's even supposed to work.

[AT] I usually do a visualization exercise with someone who is interested in Aphantasia. But it definitely is hard to explain to a neurotypical person; I think because it's so outside of their experience! I have had the pleasure of testing my mum and brother on their minds' eyes and we discovered they are also Aphants, so explaining things to them was so easy and seeing their surprise was pretty fun.

[Anonymous] I've done it a few ways: asked them to picture a sunset, asked how clear it was, then said I see nothing and discussed from there; made them read a description of Aphantasia (often Blake Ross's post) and said I have the same thing and discussed from there. Phrases that have been helpful:

- Most people have two 'screens' – the real world and the mind's eye. I only have the real world screen, that's all I see.

- Or explaining 'spatial': like being in a dark room and just *knowing* where things are, like a computer with the screen turned off (it still knows where everything is and what's happening), echolocation, Daredevil's vision, like in the Matrix where Neo sees everything in code (but non-visual), like when you're driving, and you keep an idea of the position of the cars behind you.

- All the inner senses are on a spectrum: people can visualize better or worse than others, some people don't have an inner voice, some people imagine music very well, some don't.

- How is visualizing different from a hallucination? (Answer: voluntary/involuntary, but it does get people to think. I did have to ask this in all seriousness when I first discovered Aphantasia though.)

- In reply to 'what about in situation x, do you see anything?' the answer is, no, no images *ever* when I'm awake. Nothing. I can see them when I'm asleep or the last few seconds before falling asleep, however.

*

How do people react?

[SR] Mostly mind blown. Either because they haven't thought that someone doesn't "see" – or that someone actually can!

[ND] Sometimes they are very surprised and can't imagine it. Many times they have it too. I think the percentage of people who have it is higher than some of the numbers I have seen.

[TS] Usually with surprise. I've often had people say it's the first time they've even heard of it.

[TM] People are usually shocked. They can't quite wrap their heads around what it means not to be able to see images. They often assume that I can see words but then I will correct them. They then start to imagine what that would be like for them and will explain to me what their visual world is like. I did have one person who called it a "superhero power." She felt that that must mean that other senses were really heightened, and she was correct.

[ST] They just say "Ohhh" and I don't think that they know what it means as normally they don't question it.

[SC] They are often very interested; some try to take pity on me. They sometimes think I'm playing a joke on them, but once I tell them more about it, they usually get the point.

[RH] Mostly they don't understand… and they usually get bored with the topic fairly quickly.

[MR] They usually laugh because I say my husband thought he had superpowers and they usually say something along the lines of "Well, if he does so have I" or shrug it off with "No, everyone can do that." Apart from that, they are usually disinterested. It is not something they can see or relate to, so they dismiss it.

[ML] Disbelieving mostly – unless they too cannot see pictures. But even those usually can recall smells or tastes or SOMETHING. I am the only person I know who is totally mind-blind in all the senses.

[MB2] People generally understand. I've never had anyone outright not believe me. They will often ask questions like "do you dream?" and "how do you remember how to navigate when you're driving?" I always explain that, yes, I do dream and I think I dream fairly vividly, but it's hard to say, because I can't visualize the dreams after the fact. As soon as I start to lucid dream, the dream images fall apart and become dim again.

I explain that navigating doesn't really require visualization in the same way. Anything which requires or can use motion, such as visualizing my drive to work, or how many windows I have in my house, is much easier. As long as I don't linger on images longer than a fraction of a second, and continue moving through them, I know my way around these images. If you ask me what shape is in the middle of a capital letter "A" I will physically draw the letter in my mind. The motion is the only way I could tell you that the shape is a triangle.

[JR] Some are shocked. Some wonder how I function. Others are very blasé. Depends on the person's level of curiosity, I think.

[CS] I went through a phase of asking everyone if they could visualize, and saying that I don't see anything when they can see pictures. Most people didn't believe me. A few discovered that they couldn't visualize either, they were shocked. I remembered how it made me feel when I found out, I stopped asking people after that, I think ignorance is bliss. Most people just don't understand how you can't see anything; I guess the same works in reverse though as I cannot comprehend how people can visualize things and not become confused with what is real and what is not.

[BM] Most people seem curious or even fascinated. They ask questions about it, and I answer to the best of my abilities. I always point out that there are many types of abstract concepts that we know and/or can understand without the need for mental sensory experiences – e.g., we can do mathematics, understand chemistry, understand biology, understand "fuzzy concepts", etc. all without images, sounds, etc. I say that I simply think about and negotiate my way through the world using those elements of concepts that are not dependent on mental imagery.

[Anonymous] Four ways: bemusement and little interest/great interest and shock/disbelief/confusion but interested and seeking to understand. I wonder if the different ways are related to how strong their own minds' eyes are.

*

What words of wisdom do contributors have for others when explaining the condition?

[VD] Use common sense and start small, bring up the science after.

[JS] The best way I saw it described was as a computer without a monitor. All the information is there and readily accessible but just in a different, non-visual form. The Facebook article that Blake Ross (just google Blake Ross Aphantasia) did on his Aphantasia is the most eloquent and accurate description I have found to date. It is almost exactly how my experience has gone.

[MR] People listen better if you include them personally. Tell them to close their eyes and describe a visual memory you both share, then describe your memory of it. Explain you know what happened but cannot see it in your head. If they respond positively, you can then go on to tell them other ways it affects you. Otherwise, forget it. People do not want to hear about something they can't see or understand.

[JR] Say that you are unable to pull up visual images in your mind. That you just see grey or whatever. And then say, "That's how I roll."

[MH] Get straight to the point otherwise they could think you are trying to get them to feel sorry for you. Tell them some positives at the same time because if you just focus on the negatives, guaranteed they WILL feel sorry for you.

[KB] I have never really been able to explain it very well. I know some people try and explain it like the monitor not being connected to the computer, that the information is all there and able to be accessed, it just can't be displayed. However, although this is a reasonable analogy to make, it feels like it is lacking something to my experience. I guess it makes it seem like a problem that could be simply 'fixed' by finding a way to connect the computer to the monitor. I don't see it as a problem to be fixed. I am happy just using the computer without a screen.

[JT] Keep in mind that there's no "right" way of thinking – each person has their own experience, and they are all valid ways of interacting with the world. No one is 'defective'.

[JL] Try to ask how other people are imagining things, what they see when you say something simple like "red apple" or "blue elephant"; then explain how it works for you.

[DS] The biggest issue I see is that people have trouble understanding a separation between visualizing and thinking. To them, visualizing is a major part of thinking, so the two concepts have never been thought of separately.

When describing what it's like to have a blind mind's eye, I ask them to imagine waking up tomorrow morning and realizing that they've gone blind. Can they get out of bed and make it to the bathroom? Can they get dressed? What is it about their daily activities that they can still do, but the process of doing it has now changed? Being blind is limiting, but only because they were used to seeing. Actual blind people have routines and ways of doing things that make life different, but that doesn't mean that they can't live a full and happy life. With Aphantasia, I think in a different way that doesn't depend on visualizations, but it doesn't stop me from using some other mental manipulation to understand things.

[RH] More specifically to younger Aphants: there will be things that will frustrate you, specifically in school. Others will learn it quickly, and perhaps you will struggle, but don't ever, not ever, think that this has anything to do with intelligence. You perceive and process the world a little differently than most of the people around you. Don't you worry about that. You don't have a disability; you have an advantage. I can't tell you how, or when, or even what, but someday, you'll find your advantage from your unique perspective.

As Alan makes clear, his Aphantasia is about more than visualization – it affects multiple senses. Many contributors report similar experiences.

[AK] I am unable to hear, smell, or recreate any senses in my head.

[DS] All senses are affected. I can't see, hear, smell, feel, or taste in my head.

[PW] I have Aphantasia of all senses, i.e., I cannot visualize images, sounds, smells, tastes, touches, etc. I do recall facts about all of them, but it is usually very generic unless it was a very strong experience. While I learned at an early age that I could not visualize images, and that this was not typical, it never occurred to me that my other senses were also recalled differently until I read about Aphantasia.

[GD] I have an inner ear, but no other sense – smell, touch, sight – can be recreated mentally.

[CH] I cannot recreate taste, noise, smell, or touch mentally. I do sing to myself, but words only, I don't hear full songs when suffering earworms.

[MU] All my senses are affected, except kinaesthetic.

[TS] I cannot recreate smells at all. I cannot recreate the sense of touch at all. I cannot recreate most voices or sounds. I can sometimes recreate music but even that is faint enough that I can barely hear it.

[ML] No voices, no music. I once had a very strange experience when I was under a lot of pressure/tired. I was sitting in a coffee shop and heard a group of people behind me talking in my Yorkshire uncle/aunt/cousin's voices – it was really weird. When I looked at them the voices changed to normal, but when I looked away… there it was again. It only lasted about two minutes, but I was fascinated as I could not believe that my mind could re-create a voice like that.

[TM] I feel as if my other senses are heightened due to my lack of visual skills. My auditory skills are the most attuned.

[RW] I can recreate voices and music a little bit. Usually, I need to think of a phrase and concentrate very hard, and I might be able to hear it in my head with my 'mind's ear'. I can't recreate smell/taste/touch.

[MR2] I'm not sure if other senses are affected. I'm not sure what's normal or not. I don't smell or taste things when I think of them, but my mouth waters if I think about a food that I really like. I sometimes get the melody of a song stuck in my head. To a certain extent, I can create music in my head, but it's probably more limited than for others.

[MH] I never understood until now that musicians can actually "hear" a melody in their head. Further, I learned from my colleagues that they can also "see" the notes in their mind. I chose to be an opera singer at an early age without realizing the extraordinary handicap I was facing. These are things that would be considered prerequisites and absolutely essential in order to have a professional singing career. But in my head, I hear nothing at all, ever.

The only time I can actually "hear" the melody is when my pianist is playing it at any specific moment. Then I can match the melody. At 43-years-old I've realized that all the singing I do is strictly muscle memory. And it's absolutely terrifying on stage to realize that there is no safety net of any kind if my brain stumbles on any particular part of the song. There is nothing to fall back on like "hearing" how the melody is supposed to go or "seeing" visually which notes are the correct ones.

And finally, the sense of internal rhythm is far worse than the problems with not hearing the melody. There is no sense of remembering how a previous beat went in order to anticipate the next beat. Thus there is no way to regulate internally the passing of time which is essential to making music. This is by far the worst because I can get by somewhat by not hearing the melody. For instance, my accompanist will oftentimes play my melody part along with the piano part of the song and most people in the audience won't be able to realize that she is helping me.

[Anonymous] My other senses are also affected. The only sound I can hear in my head is my own voice. No music or other voices. I can get a song stuck in my head though, but then I just hear my own voice singing the song (either the lyrics or instrumental). I also can't smell or taste anything in my head.

[JS] I cannot recreate audio in my head. No memories of taste either.

[L] I now refer to my experience as "Like Helen Keller in my head." I'm blind, deaf, dumb and mute!

[KB] I very very rarely hear music in my mind, and as soon as I focus on it, the music stops. I never recreate voices.

[JK2] I can't recreate audio in my head in the same way that I originally heard it. When I "sing" or narrate in my head, it's basically my own voice mimicking the qualities of what I heard. If the singer had a gravelly voice, then I "hear" my own voice with that gravelly quality. Interestingly, my brain seems to "pretend" to make my throat do whatever it needs to in order to make the sound even if it's not a sound I could possibly make, like an eagle scream or a horse neigh.

Recreating instrumental music in my head is literally just my own internal voice going "Dum Dum Dum..." and I can only focus on one instrument at a time. However, I do remember the feelings that the music or voice evokes when I hear them for real.

I can't recall smells at all, but I can recall words for them. I know that lilac is a "soft" scent that makes my toes tingle; it reminds me of my mother and summer mountain sunshine. I know the scent of rotting chicken is vile, and I might even shudder at the thought of it, but I don't smell it.

[CS2] All my other senses are affected too. Even though I have known about Aphantasia for about a year now, it was only a couple of months ago that I realized that people can also recreate other senses in their mind – "visualize" a smell, a taste, or a sound. That blew my mind for a second time.

I can recreate different melodies of songs in my head, but it's very "quiet" and not in the voice of whoever sings it. I can't recreate voices, or the specific sound of an instrument. For example, I can think of the melody to Bohemian Rhapsody, even the guitar solos, but it doesn't sound like Freddy Mercury, and the guitar doesn't sound like a guitar – I couldn't imagine what it would sound like if someone was playing it on a flute, or a saxophone.

I am completely unable to "visualize" smells, tastes, and tactile information.

Chapter 3: Early Years

As human beings grow up, we gradually develop the characteristics, personality traits, abilities and preferences that help to define us as individuals. However, a simple question has troubled scientists for generations: are we the products of our inherited genes or our environments?

One of the reasons scientists are so interested in the nature vs. nurture debate is because the answer can allow us to understand and potentially even predict human behaviour.

While the nature vs. nurture debate has raged on for centuries, more recent research has confirmed that, in reality, both nature and nurture are relevant for most things (simply to greater and lesser degrees, rather than wholly). Generally speaking, as we grow up, both our upbringing and our genetics seem to play a roughly equal role in determining how we develop and what characteristics we have.

In 2015, a comprehensive analysis of almost every twin study carried out in the last 50 years found that both genetics and environmental factors contribute roughly equally to human traits. The reason twin studies are so important in this field is because twins develop from the same egg and share the same genome. This means that, if environmental factors did not play a role, identical twins should grow up to share all traits, regardless of how they were reared and whether they were raised together or apart. Yet, five decades worth of research shows this is not the case, and twins can develop in substantially different ways.

Cross-cultural evidence, for example, highlights the fact that sexual preferences have a largely genetic basis whilst, similarly, a number of psychological traits are influenced more by genetics than environment. Other human traits develop primarily as a result of the environment we grow up in, rather than being genetically pre-determined. One example of this is sense of humour (primarily a learned trait influenced by a person's cultural environment and the people they are raised by, rather than being inherited). Meanwhile, a combination of genetics and environment contribute towards intelligence; a 2011 study from Washington University in St. Louis found that a child's intelligence is significantly influenced by maternal support, and other research has highlighted a link between activities like playing a musical instrument and academic intelligence.

Whilst it is too early to determine the exact influences of genes and the environment on people with Aphantasia, one thing is clear – childhood is a commonly-held event(!) throughout which people have different experiences and influences.

*

[Alan] When I look back through my school reports one of the recurring themes throughout all my years at school was the phrase, "Alan appears to daydream." I know I did because I have read it in my school reports; they say so, and my parents told me I did. But I have no memories of what I used to daydream about. Has my ability changed over the years or do I have the same ability to daydream? Is it just more difficult to access the memories for the daydreaming process?

I should try to remember when I first realized I couldn't imagine.

Obviously, recalling a memory that goes so far into the past is not easy, but I think I remember how, in the UK in the 1970's (1976), there was a television programme called "The Fall and Rise of Reginald Perrin." The programme was about the peculiar behaviour of the eponymous Perrin, a man bored by his job. Anyway, Perrin used to imagine his mother-in-law as an animal – a hippopotamus. He'd always see footage of a scampering hippopotamus in his head when he thought of her, and that's when I first wondered 'Why can't I do that?' That is possibly the earliest moment from which I started to think others could see something I couldn't. I never realized at the time that it didn't make that much sense, so I just dismissed it as something on TV. Something where a television programme showed something that wasn't possible.

I do not have as many times as well defined as the Reginald Perrin memory; times when I could have really questioned what I could see in my mind. It seems now, perhaps, that as a child or whilst growing up, I did not consider what actually happened in my mind – I just accepted it.

At secondary school, we used to have drama lessons under the guidance of a teacher called Mr. Templar. In one of the lessons, he asked us to pretend to be animals, and to spend some of the lesson moving around the drama studio as that animal. I never understood what we were supposed to do, as I could imagine nothing in my mind. I just did the same as the others without really knowing that they could imagine things I could never see.

My long term memory is quite poor from my school days and I have limited information accessible from it. But I am aware of times when I felt confused and did things just to copy others, simply because I had no mental imaginary to access and use in the real world. It's only now that I understand this.

*

The effect of Aphantasia on people during their early years and schooldays can be challenging to unravel; simply because most people did not know about the condition or that many of their peers and siblings were able to visualize. Did Aphantasia affected people's schooldays?

[ND] It didn't. I have always been a very good student.

[CS] I don't know. I never knew I was any different from anyone else. I just got on with life.

[AK] I have no idea because I don't know any other way. I was a bright student, relatively successful. In hindsight, having the capacity to recreate images in the mind would perhaps have made learning easier but judging by what I now know about Aphants maybe I have compensatory abilities. It seems to me that most of the Aphants in the group are relatively intelligent and successful so who knows?

[Anonymous] I don't think it did – I was a very good student. I was quite shy, but not sure if I can reliably link that to Aphantasia. I was a creative intellectual sort of student – I did English, Biology, Calculus, Graphics (design, architecture, technical drawing) and French in my last year of high school. I'm very good at thinking in 3D.

[TS] Arts class was hell. The teacher always gave us a topic and a technique and showed us an example picture that we weren't actually allowed to mimic though. And then told us to start working.

Without an existing reference I couldn't draw worth a damn. Everything always looked like it was drawn like a five-year-old. Nothing ever had the right proportions since I never had a mental picture to compare against.

The only two times I managed to draw an actually good picture were the two times when we actually had a reference to draw from. The first time, we had to replicate an existing picture and the second time we had to draw a portrait of the person sitting in front of us.

Also, I never got any advantage from drawing mind maps. They were always just sillier looking bullet point lists to me.

[L] I never knew I had it during school. I struggled in math and marvelled at kids who could complete the times table in under six minutes in sixth grade. (I contemplate that now and think they could visualize the answers, compared to me who had to memorize them or do the math.)

I was very creative, artistic, good at English, and writing. I hated reading novels and bought Cliff notes for the books that were assigned and always got A's. I had to memorize spelling words and did fine.

I have often remembered an incident in German language class in high school when the teacher called my attention back to the room as I was staring out the window, "Stop watching the monkeys climbing on the trees and get back to work!" I often wondered what he meant by that and thought it was weird. It was so weird that I remember it to this day!

Now that I know that I was different – a non-visualizer – I can associate many things to that, but I made it through in my own way.

[JR] I was an excellent student; my specialties included spelling (in grade school I even got 100% for a quarter or semester because I got 100% on every spelling test). I wasn't very good with geography; still aren't. And chemistry. OMG, I was so lucky I had good partners in high school and college.

I was terrible in geometry in high school; I got headache during a lot of those classes. But, I loved and did well in algebra. I learned French and had a decent accent.

Aphantasia didn't affect me studying; I didn't take copious notes, just the salient points. I memorized things I needed to for tests or whatever. I was always good at making connections between things. I won writing contests. Though shy, I was a leader.

[JT] I had difficulty with geography, and foreign languages, which makes a lot of sense now, as visualization would have been a helpful tool in both. History had too many names and dates for me. Math and science were easy as I could conceptualize things (although math always had to be done on paper or I had to work very hard to commit something to rote memory).

English I was good in, as a big part of my thinking is in stories (although I skip long, visually descriptive paragraphs when reading, as well as when I write). Because I read a lot, I am a good speller, though not because I can "see" how something should be spelled. If I write something down, I "know" if it is right or wrong – kind of like recognizing people when I encounter them again, even if I couldn't describe them without actually seeing them. I also did well in art, except when trying to draw something I am not actually looking at.

[LH] I didn't know why at the time but I could never draw anything unless I had a picture of it in front of me. I found it very difficult when asked to do a piece of creative writing where you had to imagine a place or scene and write about it.

[MB] I didn't know I had it, my education seemed normal to me. I was always the cleverest kid in the class; school came easy to me.

[AS] I remember sometimes on worksheets or exercises where the teacher would tell us to close our eyes and imagine such-and-such. I always had a little trouble concentrating during these types of exercises because I could never actually "see" anything. I assumed no one else did either. I mean, I know what a beach looks like and I can describe it, so I would just think about those things. But no picture appeared.

[TM] I was horrible at spelling and math. It took me a while to learn how to read because I don't think I could easily remember the patterns of letters. However, once I broke that code I could hardly be stopped when it came to reading.

Due to early learning troubles, I grew to think that I wasn't as smart as other people. It took me until midway through my sophomore year of college to really become a learner. By the time I got to grad school, I had figured out a system and graduated with a 4.0. It took a lot to think of myself as intelligent. To this day I can doubt myself because of my early learning issues.

[VD] I never felt it, but in hindsight the way I remember things tends to correlate with the fields I did better in (science, math, history) and possibly explains my shortcomings in others (I have never appreciated fiction so English was rough; geometry frustrated me because I couldn't do a lot of the work mentally like I do in algebra).

In retrospect, in first grade, I was rebuked for not participating in an exercise meant to clear the mind. I opened my eyes, told her I couldn't see the beach she was talking about, and she told me to participate and try (she didn't know any better). As an older child (maybe 15), I felt that people saw things differently, but just chalked it up to being a weird kid.

[RH] Rote memorization – I couldn't stand it, couldn't do it. Flash cards did nothing for me… now I know why.

[JC] Looking back, I found it easier to remember things by rote. I have never been able to learn all my times tables no matter how hard I try.

[MR2] For the most part, school subjects were easy for me unless they required memorization. I struggled significantly with Geography to the point that I barely passed the class, but it didn't seem to cause problems for any of my classmates. I initially thought that we had a difficult teacher, but I couldn't understand how the class could be easy for everyone else. I also had difficulty with art since I couldn't picture anything in my mind and I lacked creativity.

[AT] Weirdly, I was always in trouble for daydreaming! I don't recall that I ever imagined images when I was zoned out, I think I just liked drifting away with my thoughts. I was a great student though, once I focussed. I do wish I'd known about Aphantasia when I was doing my GCSEs. It might have made studying easier – I could've worked around it instead of trying to force myself to use teacher-prescribed methods.

[BM] It affected me very little as far as I know. The only thing I can remember is that I had a hard time memorizing the multiplication table. The idea of one number at one end of a column combining with a number at one end of a row to produce what seemed like a random third number was incomprehensible to me. The teachers told us to memorize the multiplication table, and I now interpret that as 'see the table in your mind'. I had to teach myself what the multiplication table actually meant and then to do quick calculations that made sense. For example, I taught myself that 6x8 is not just simply 48. It is actually two instances of three 8s (=24+24), as well as three instances of two 8s (=16+16+16), as well as four instances of two 6s (=12+12+12+12), etc. Since I could not simply see the table in my head, I had to develop another strategy which made the details of the task and the internal relationships among the numbers explicit.

[MC] I understand now why I didn't "get" mental math. It was a very mysterious — and impossible — concept for me. At the time, I didn't know (and my teachers didn't know) that I was missing the key component for that process.

[MH] Not sure exactly, still trying to figure that out.

[ST] Reading was always slow and hard work.

[ML] I cannot remember dates and facts, they just don't stay with me. That has got to be the worst thing in a learning environment. However, I'm a voracious reader having, I think, been born with the ability to read. I don't remember a time when I couldn't read. This was a great way of filling the void which I now realize 'sighted' people don't have in their heads. Being a reader, I picked up tons of information which just floats around and 'pops up' when I need it. So although I don't have access to facts and figures, I do have good intuitional leaps, so can keep ahead of the game most of the time.

[MU] No memory of events. My friend in second grade asked me what was wrong with my memory. It was impossible to remember historical dates. Math was difficult.

[PW] It mostly did not, as my form of "visualizing" is patterns and concepts, which made math, science, and grammar easy, plus I have a great memory for things I read.

There were some things that were annoyances in retrospect though. For instance, I had to make my teacher keep repeating the proper spelling when we would swap papers to grade each other's quizzes, and it was annoying for her as much as for me since we both knew I could spell them all correctly. But I couldn't track more than a few letters she was saying at a time when I was simultaneously trying to check someone else's paper.

[SB] I was really bad at geometry (because I struggle with visual thinking), also art class wasn't that great but otherwise, it didn't affect me much because I found ways of studying that worked for me.

[SC] I didn't find out about Aphantasia until I had finished school. Looking back, it definitely played a part in me failing my English classes. I was great at English until I was required to visualize. I would be asked to write a short story, and I would, but when I never put any description of imagery, the teachers would give me low marks. Because I had no use for imagery while reading a book, I never included any in my writing.

I was horrible at spelling. I could tell right away if a word was spelt right, or if it was incorrect, but if I spelt something wrong, I wouldn't be able to correct it.

*

Looking back (when growing up), 'disconnects' can be thought of as times when a person's endeavours and understanding were somewhat out of kilter with what they saw and experienced around them. Some disconnects can leave a lasting impression although, naturally, the root causes may originate from any number of sources. Not necessarily Aphantasia.

[JR] My first real disconnect was when taking an IQ test prior to high school. I was about 13. Part of the test, as you know, is 'spatial reasoning skills'. I was completely stymied. So, I walked up to the tester and said, "I don't know what they want me to do for this section." She said, "Just read the directions." Not helpful.

I guessed at all the answers. I know now that my inability to do this task was a result of my Aphantasia. This definition makes sense as to why I would have trouble with these skills.

[ML] When all the other teenage girls were going through the hero/singer/actor worship, I could not 'get it'. I couldn't fall in love with someone I'd never met, or swoon over a picture. I tried hard to fake it but gave up in the end. I can only interact with something that is 'there'. I don't have any reality for something 'made-up' like crushes.

[JA] [Disconnects] describe my whole life. It makes me laugh, but it's true.

I struggle with humankind as a whole. I know there are decent people, but I honestly feel humans are corrupt and selfish. I regularly think about living in the woods with just pets and my child. I love people dearly, so much it hurts…

We humans tend to value things that I feel do not matter: success, material possessions, physical beauty, popularity and countless other things that aren't true and which we will leave behind when we pass away. People have so many demands and expectations from everyone else and do very little self-improvement or even honest self-reflection.

[PW] I was always told that I had little common sense even though I was very smart. I think looking back that it was a disconnect that I was "seeing" things the same way as others.

[MH] My voice teacher said I was the hardest working student he ever had and I made little to zero improvement in musicianship skills... ear training, sight singing, pitches, etc.

The one and only thing I excelled in (and still do) is the vocal apparatus itself comprising all the muscular intricacies of a solid vocal laryngeal technique.

Most of my life has been not getting what I worked for and was 'supposed to'. Not all having to do with Aphantasia though.

[Anonymous] I realized at about age 15 that I wasn't as good at remembering faces as everyone else was – this was from watching TV/movies where I'd sometimes have to ask who people were because I didn't recognize them from a previous scene (e.g., especially short brown-haired white males).

[TM] I don't know if I felt different due to Aphantasia, as I didn't know that others had an ability I didn't. I did know that I was not the learner that my friends and siblings were. I just thought that I wasn't as intelligent and would get super frustrated because I took so much longer to do homework or tests.

[RW] Not really. I've always kind of 'rolled with it'. Take meditation; now I understand that my experience of it has been completely hollow, but at the time I just assumed that the whole point was to think of some nice stuff. I just thought it affected some people more than others. I've accepted early that things affect everyone in different ways, so I shrugged it off.

[JT] Looking back, it was always odd to me when people would say – when watching a movie after reading a book –

that the character wasn't how they "pictured" them. I never had a problem with that.

[L] I have no timing! From elementary school through to high school, I was terrible at cheerleading, acting on stage, keeping rhythm and timing. I was often shamed for this.

At age 11, I taught myself to play the guitar, and I wrote my own songs from the beginning because I could not play other songs in time. I persisted in composing, playing and singing in restaurants, competitions, weddings and entered contests. I was good at it, but now I look back after learning about Aphantasia, I realize that other people actually hear music in their heads, they can count in their heads, they see images in their heads. I don't know how I did it, but it was a passion.

[MU] I have always been avoidant of seeing people I might know in public places, fearing I would not remember/recognize them and that they would be uncomfortable. This goes back to childhood.

[LH] Paper folding activities in school would have me in tears because I would forget what to do. Movement has always been difficult for me, e.g., dancing and following actions as I am always behind and cannot keep up or remember any of the steps.

[TM] Sometimes, when directions were given in multiple steps, I would get super confused. I could see that other people knew how to do what was being asked. I just couldn't make sense of how it worked.

[JK2] I also have problems with abstracts. As a child, I was faced with five items – four were various desserts, and one was a vegetable, and I had to pick the one that didn't belong. I couldn't answer it because every single item was different – one had crust, one had a cone, one had a cherry... at no point did I realize that the difference was that one was a vegetable.

Likewise, I have trouble anticipating complex patterns, like in an IQ test where it shows (to me) random and unrelated shapes and wants me to draw the next shape. I have no idea what the next shape could be – it could be anything!

[RH] Spelling – I just couldn't get it. Thank god for technology and spellcheck everywhere! I really struggled with memorizing anything without context. A list of history dates, memorizing countries, states, multiplication tables – forget it. I either worked really really hard, or bombed!

[DG] How did I get through life – without realizing something was 'not right'? Why was it never picked up by anyone else?

*

In line with the idea of disconnects, the impact of Aphantasia on early relationships – with siblings and peers in particular – piques a lot of interest. Of course, in line with 'disconnects' (above) many people may feel different to peers and family for reasons that have nothing to do with Aphantasia.

[RH] I did feel different, but I didn't know why.

[DS] I've always felt different. I think that's normal and had nothing to do with Aphantasia.

[LH] I have always felt different to most people in life but was never sure why. I don't know how much of this is related to Aphantasia.

[JA] Yes, my brother is extremely intelligent. He was reading encyclopaedias and adult books by age eight while I read picture books and struggled to finish those. I grew up thinking I was stupid. I have always felt different.

[MB] I have always felt a bit different. I think more than most people seem to.

[RW] I think just, in ways, everyone feels a bit lonely sometimes? I felt like socializing has always been a bit cumbersome to me, but I think that's just a bit of social anxiety and not Aphantasia. So I guess, not more than most people to the best of my knowledge.

[ST] My oldest brother was really bright and talented and learned really fast and excelled at school, playing Chess, piano, etc. And I noticed that my Math teacher was hoping that I would be just as talented as my brother – I had to disappoint him.

[CS] No, not at all. I don't feel any different now either.

[MC] No, I didn't feel any different from my sibling or friends. I didn't know I was any different in that regard.

[ML] Not really, some of my siblings can't 'see' either. My best friend does, and I do feel different in that she gets very emotional and misses people and stuff.

[PA] No. My father was a painter and photographer, and my sister became an architect. We were surrounded by images. They were in my head, and I have strong visual memory, but I cannot "see" them with my eyes closed.

[PW] Not because of Aphantasia, although now I realize that a lot of social awkwardness is probably due as much or more to Aphantasia as to being introverted.

[MR2] I lacked an imagination and I didn't enjoy anything that required make-believe or creativity. I often didn't enjoy the same things as most of the other kids my age did and as a result was often left out.

[BM] I was good at some things, which set me apart from some peers, and I was bad at some things, which set me apart from some peers. I ultimately came out as bisexual, so that also caused me to feel different, and I came from a poor, single-parent home, which also caused me to feel different.

However, I never felt different because I did not have pictures, sounds, smells, etc. in my mind.

[TS] Not due to Aphantasia. I was always 'the smart kid' so most of the difference came from that.

[Anonymous] Possibly some bemusement at make-believe games, but not enough that it stopped me playing them with others or by myself. Apart from being shy, I don't think so?

[JK2] I was unaware that I had a different imaginative experience from others. I have always been described as having an over-active imagination and being highly creative, so Aphantasia didn't affect me negatively there.

[JK] No because I haven't experienced anything other than Aphantasia so it doesn't make me feel different.

[L] I have three sisters, two older and one younger. I didn't/don't feel different but can realize many things that were/are different now that I know I am different in my blackness. I have asked them and they are all visualizers. One is a graphic designer, another a landscape designer, the other always has grandiose ideas about designing her home(s). Her husband calls it the big "V" as in vision!

Chapter 4: Imagination

Popular definitions of imagination often relate to both creativity and imagery, although it is self-evident that people can be creative without the need for imagery and visualization. In some ways, imagination can be considered as the reverse process to perception where events are processed (using the senses), cognitively evaluated, and memories subsequently laid down.

Imagination, by comparison, sees internally-held information being reprocessed and repackaged to create innovative thoughts, outcomes, and solutions to questions and deliberations. Progressing beyond this cognitive stage (to creating sensory perceptions and representations) is not a necessity.

Imagination is often shaped by personal experiences and also heavily influenced during childhood.

*

[Alan] I know I have an imagination, but surely that would be incompatible with not being able to visualize anything in my mind? I think that an imagination is much more than just imagery. I believe, in my case, it's my mental ability to consider complex scenarios. Okay, I can't imagine monsters, nightmare animals, or things like that when I am awake, but I think my imagination is more targeted towards ideas and problem-solving.

According to one definition, imagination is: "The faculty or action of forming new ideas, or images or concepts of external objects not present to the senses."

As a small child, I had a massive imagination, and would often scare myself thinking about what was under the bed, in the wardrobe, and all the other usual places. I have to say, my parents never found anything after I insisted they check. I guess I could never split the world into things in my mind and those in the real world – to me they only happened in the real world.

I really wanted to enjoy reading books for personal pleasure, but I never really could. Although I like reading fiction, I can't visualize the written stories, so I always struggle with the words on the page. Reading the words doesn't create the visual imagery necessary to follow the story or even to understand the characters.

To explain how I have to read books, I have to read the paragraphs two or three times depending on the complexity of the story and number of characters. I also have to sit and ponder what some of the words mean, and it can take a while before I get what is happening. Progress depends on how many words are on the page. Often, when I then turn the page over, I will almost immediately forget what I have just read; my mind just goes totally blank and I have to reread the page to see if I can remember it enough to turn the page over again.

I seem to be able to follow factual stories more easily than fictional ones.

What does the difference between fiction and non-fiction really mean? It means I can find it easier to read the book of a story if I have already seen it as a television programme. Or as a film that closely matches the story. The story doesn't have to be exactly the same but it has to be close enough for me to make the connections in my mind. This is probably the opposite of what people normally want. They usually want to read the book first then see the movie afterwards, but I know that would not work for me.

I am able to read some books but the amount of effort required is probably inversely proportional to the previous knowledge I have with the story/book I am trying to read. If I have a good understanding of the plot and characters then I am more likely to be able to read with a certain ease; but, if I know little about the plot or characters then I may not get past the first chapter and just give up in frustration. I guess, in essence, there is not a rigid rule about what I can read, but I know my limitations based on my previous experiences and struggles.

*

One thing that shone through from the contributors to this book is how imaginative and creative many Aphants are. Others, conversely, feel that they have limited imaginations.

[MB2] I think I have a great imagination and I don't think Aphantasia affects it. Before I knew I had Aphantasia, it didn't even occur to me that imagination could be visual process. I just thought of concepts in a more abstract sense, and mentally added other elements or concepts to it as my imagination allowed. No images necessary.

They are non-visual. Ideas and concepts instead of images. I can often visualize a schematic of my ideas, sort of like flowcharts, or Venn diagrams – essentially a spatial organization of ideas. But these are simple and non-vivid images, which I think makes all the difference. There are never any physical colours or intricate shapes in my imagination – these ideas are always just 'ideas'.

[JR] I think my strengths in this area are coming up with new ways of doing things, being able to fly by the seat of my pants (when speaking, doing research, dealing with people, etc.) I'm a critical thinker, too. I like to philosophize.

I am good at problem-solving, and thinking of new ideas and in communicating with others; both verbally and in writing. I'm also very curious, which I think is helpful. I love trying new things.

[VD] I have a good imagination. Aphantasia may affect it but not much or only in certain ways (I can't put my imagination onto paper as a drawing to save my life).

[PA] I work as a film director and screenwriter. I tell stories and make films, and they are based on the things I remember from reality and other films and images and books. I am good at using bits and parts from here and there and creating new meaning.

[L] I have a great imagination! I am very creative. I definitely know that my blackness affects it because I cannot see what I am trying to create. I guess I go by feeling balanced in the way things are together.

I go by instinct and inspiration. When I am designing for a client, I get ideas like thoughts. I have learned to go with the "ideas" and follow them. It has been very successful.

[MR] I have a very good imagination for stories. I write stories and poems and have had many published. It works fine in the written and verbal spheres. I cannot imagine how something in the real world should look. E.g., I cannot imagine how a room would look if I added elements, or how a piece of artwork would look if I put it together.

[MU] I have a very good imagination, but it is primarily verbal. I am a poet and writer of other things.

I am unusually stimulated by visual experiences, such as being in nature and observing artistic or natural beauty. My response is much more dramatic than anyone else I have ever met. I think it is because seeing the natural world is always a shock!

[PW] I have a great imagination for concepts and patterns, and thus for things that are philosophical or abstractions – but obviously I cannot visualize images. Thus I am not fond of Aphantasia being described as lacking imagination, or even a "mind's eye" – it is a lack of sensory visualization.

It manifests in terms of concepts and patterns. I can easily solve puzzles and navigate and anything abstract. I am also very skilled as a software developer, typically finding easier solutions than most.

[AT] I am an author and an artist, so my imagination is pretty active. I'm about to start working on a painting that I imagined in descriptive words; when I paint it, I will need to use a reference model, and I work on a trial and error system where I am constantly adjusting as the picture appears on canvas – because that's the first time I'm seeing it!

[RW] I'm good at coming up with concepts and ideas, and making connections. I'm good at developing those concepts.

[AK] Not a good imagination but some imagination. I have to work at imagining something like a step-by-step process. I imagine it would be better if it just arrived in picture or movie format... but it doesn't. It's more theoretical, reasoned.

[JA] I always thought I did, but I laugh now because I realize creativity and imagination are different. I love sci-fi movies because I can SEE them, but sci-fi books are really difficult for me to read because I cannot visualize the world. I have extremely vivid, colourful, and sometimes disturbing dreams.

[AS] I used to think I did, but now I'm not so sure. My mom always told me I had quite the imagination, and I guess I did come up with some crazy scenarios for my Barbies or things like that. But I don't have the vivid imagination that my son has. So, I think Aphantasia definitely affects it.

[JK2] I think [my imagination] relies heavily on concepts. I create an invisible "set" in the blackness of my mind, complete with invisible actors. I then use words and concepts to bring it to life. Words come strapped with all kinds of baggage – and it's not all visual. So my invisible set might be in a "seedy nightclub" complete with all of the feelings, sounds and smells (that I neither smell nor hear, but know would be there) that come with those two words.

I then use words to make the scene play out.

"Stan leaps over the second story railing, dropping heavily to the first floor and knocking over a chair as he staggers forward..." while mentally moving the invisible "Stan" character from point A to B. It's hard to describe, but works just fine for me. This is also how books play out in my head.

[AY] [My imagination is] pretty good. But I've found that I cannot create something new if I'm doing art; I can only copy things.

[GD] It allows for me to put things together that most of my visual thinking friends say they would never think of.

[GD] [My imagination manifests as] characters, plots, imaginary adventurers mostly in Role Playing games.

[JK] My imagination is okay, but I'm not a creative person.

[MH] What I do have is very impulsive and spontaneous and almost always consists of exaggerated humour. Does Aphantasia affect it? Yes, Aphantasia doesn't let me weight the pros and cons of what I imagine and let me "play them out" beforehand.

[ML] Lousy imagination, I think it's because I can't see pictures, and so cannot create anything. I'm reasonable at creating craft things, but cannot ever repeat the item. I cannot remember how to do it. All my creations are one-offs because they are hit and miss affairs.

[MR2] I feel that I have no imagination.

[JS] I think of the word or scenario and associate verbs to describe it.

[MC] Just thoughts – words, concepts, conversations, ideas. I do not fantasize or daydream. My use of imagination tends to be factual and intentional, mostly for making plans.

[ST] I interlink new information with old info, and have a wondering questioning mind, and might come up with a new idea/concept.

[TM] For me it manifests in narrative form. It is auditory, and it pulls from things that I have read, heard, or watched recently.

[TS] I can come up with an idea for a pretty skirt. I won't actually see if my idea works until I've sewn it so I often have to make changes at that point.

[ND] I can conjure up all kinds of insane scenarios. I simply don't see them.

*

"Although I like reading fiction," wrote Alan, "I can't visualize the written stories, so I always struggle with the words on the page." How does Aphantasia affect people's enjoyment of books and reading?

[MU] I don't enjoy reading fiction. I have NO inner experience of writers' descriptions of what things look like, and it is impossible for me to follow complicated plotlines.

[CS] I do not enjoy overly descriptive books, I get lost and have to read the paragraph over and over. Some books I really enjoy though. I think this is why I enjoy it when they come out on film because I can 'see' the words come to life. I absorb non-fiction with no problem at all.

[AK] Perhaps it affects the type of books I like to read. As with others, long descriptions of visuals bore me.

[KB] I LOVE reading fiction books. I get completely involved in the stories and characters. I especially love science fiction like Lord of the Rings and Harry Potter.

[L] I do not like fiction, especially the long descriptions of the physical characteristics of characters. I enjoy science and spiritual books. If I do not get the concepts, I contemplate. I enjoyed learning about Einstein and his thought experiments as a Theoretical Physicist. I certainly don't have the math, but I can explore magnificent concepts in thought. Likewise, I enjoy reading about Nikola Tesla, Buckminster Fuller and Edgar Cayce. My design ideas are not as grand as cosmic explorations, but I believe my ability is from the same realm of energy that other's abilities come from, just different.

[JC] I enjoy reading but I speed read over the descriptive passages. It also means that when a film is made of a book – I enjoy it since I don't have a great deal of detailed scenery in my head. So, for example, I enjoyed the Harry Potter films after reading the books as they helped my imagination to enjoy the scenery as well as the story.

[TS] All descriptive text is nearly useless to me and I mentally just skip it. The parts I care about are the action and the dialogue.

[AS2] I love reading books and read at least a book or more a week, but I cannot imagine scenes and what people look like unless I see a film of the book afterwards.

[MR] I love books. I don't visualize the descriptions but mentally accept them as part of the story.

[MR2] I enjoy reading fictional books, but I prefer to read something that doesn't have lengthy descriptions or jumps around a lot between timeframes, characters, etc. I often prefer books that are written for middle schoolers rather than adults. Also, if there are multiple books in a series, I prefer to wait until the entire series is available and read all of the books back to back. If I have to wait several months to a year between books, I'll need to reread the ones that I've already read as I'll have forgotten most of the book. Non-fiction is too dry and boring, and I'll lose interest fairly quickly. Also, if there are too many descriptive words, I'll lose interest in the book and quit reading it.

[JK2] I love books. I have been an avid reader since I was able to string letters together into words. I lived in the library most summers during my childhood. I am striving to be a fiction writer myself. If I could be paid to just read books all day, I would do it (instead, I am paid to be a librarian). I would say Aphantasia hasn't affected my ability to enjoy books at all. Granted, it might be cool to experience the story visually as well, but I don't feel like I'm missing out.

I prefer fiction, and in fiction I have a preference for fantasy and science fiction. Non-fiction is dry and sterile while fiction is alive and moving.

[JL] I read a lot and love reading books, but dislike long and detailed descriptions (my mind gets overloaded by them and I simply skip them automatically, without realizing). I like simple and short descriptions (that helps me to set up the world). However, books with mostly dialogue and a lack of descriptions are tiresome.

Mostly I read fiction, as it's more fun. I never considered this preference was connected with imagination.

[MC] I love reading and always have. I had no idea that the mental images are often the main thing that most people get out of reading a book. I tend to skip over lengthy descriptions of non-characters in fiction though (landscapes, buildings, rooms, clothing, physical appearance, etc.). The lengthy, minute details are of no use to me; I get by with an understanding of the basic visual attributes of a person or place. I prefer fiction. I live in the real world and experience real world things. Since I mostly read for enjoyment, I prefer to read about things other than the real world.

[Anonymous] I'm a bit sad that I can't see mind's eye movies of what's happening, but something is happening in my head, and I can definitely get lost in a book. I prefer fast-paced, character-driven, thought-provoking novels with twists, though I will read and enjoy more literary or classic works. I read a lot of Young Adult fiction (which tends to be fast-paced, character-driven and thought-provoking). I have to read poetry at least twice before it starts to make sense.

I'm a bookworm. As a child, my friends would get annoyed when I went over to play with them and started reading their books instead. My mother (a visualizer) is also a bookworm.

I read far more fiction than non-fiction, probably because fiction is an escape and non-fiction seems like work. That said, when I do read non-fiction I'm pleasantly surprised by how much I enjoy it and wonder why I don't read more. So perhaps I'm a little prejudiced against it for some reason.

[AY] I cannot read certain authors because of their style of writing. I won't read Asimov because he spends a lot of time describing things, and I usually gloss over stuff like that when I read. I never know what any of the characters or locations are supposed to look like, but I don't care either. I just enjoy reading.

[MH] Reading is painful. I don't remember what I read. It seems for every 8-10 words I might get a flash of an idea of what a quarter of those words mean.

[DS] I don't enjoy reading, especially fiction. I have a large audiobook collection because I love consuming books, but I don't want to physically read them.

[BM] I started reading when I was very young, and I have been an avid reader my entire life. I love "disappearing" into a book. When I read, I lose conscious awareness of the real world, and an alternative world forms in my mind – not with pictures, sounds, etc., but it is very rich anyway.

74

I prefer fiction because it makes me think about and form connections among things that I otherwise might not have thought about or put together. It helps me to conceptualize alternative realities and alternative points of view, and it helps me to consider alternative emotions in different circumstances. I am an academic and read a lot of non-fiction for work. That is enjoyable on a professional level, but it does not provide the same opportunity to expand my horizons on a personal/emotional/creative level.

[AS] [Aphantasia] doesn't affect it at all. I have always LOVED reading. I get really caught up in books, which was kind of surprising to some people after they found out I couldn't visualize anything. I do think Aphantasia must help me to read faster though. My husband takes forever to read books. I can sit and read a book in a day, or even an afternoon, if it really draws me in.

I listen to podcasts mostly. I love podcasts, especially true crime.

[RH] [Podcasts] Yes, all the time. I listen during my commute to and from work, about 1.5 hours, daily. I also sometimes listen as I am going to sleep.

[CS2] [Podcasts] all the time! Anytime I'm alone and doing any mindless task – even for one or two minutes – I put on a podcast. That's how I found out about Aphantasia – I had to do some gardening, so guess what? Podcast. I have never tried audiobooks, though.

[DG] I've only really thought about this [Aphantasia and enjoying books] recently. I have no visualization but I can 'feel' it – but not visually.

[JR] I enjoy many types of books including fiction. When I read descriptions, I make a cursory attempt to 'picture' the scene, but I don't really see anything. It hasn't interfered with my enjoyment of books. The good thing is that when books are turned into movies, I don't have any preconceived notions regarding what the characters look like, etc.

I am curious about the world around me and always asking questions, so non-fiction is great. I enjoy fiction if it's a good story; I can enjoy a story immensely without 'seeing' anything in my mind's eye.

[ML] I am a voracious reader – if I have to sit around or go on a journey then I must have my books or my audio books. Most times, I will have a few books on the go all at the same time. I remember the storylines etc. well. My memory for words is very good.

Audio books all the time. I would not drive my car to town without my books. They are on my mobile phone, and I play them on earphones or on Bluetooth.

[SB] [Aphantasia and enjoying books] It doesn't really affect me. I've always loved reading, and it's similar to me trying to remember something from day-to-day life. I know the facts (for example, that a character has brown hair) but I just can't see it, or sometimes I can imagine little things like the length of their hair. But that's seldom the case.

[TM] I was a slow learner when it came to reading. Once I figured it out, I was pretty much unstoppable. I read more than most people I know. When I read, I can easily have a few books going at one time. I tend to be a very fast reader, perhaps because my mind isn't creating the images to go with it. Unlike many people, I have no problem rereading books. I think I pull more from books every time I read them.

I am CONSTANTLY listening to podcasts and I adore audiobooks. Silence is really hard for me, so I like to fill any quiet/alone time with podcasts. They make a great platform for learning new information and constantly challenging my thinking.

[AR] As I have become more aware of Aphantasia, I have been trying harder to try and conjure an image [when reading]; I do occasionally manage to create a visual image, although it is brief.

[AS2] [Sometimes, words on a page can create images] but I believe the images are from things that I've actually experienced. For example, I can visualize a beach that is referred to in a book as I've regularly been on one. However, if the book described scenery, I am unlikely to be able to imagine it.

Chapter 5: Visual imagery

The biological underpinnings of visualization were covered, briefly, at the start of this book. Studies with children have shown that visual imagery is a key component utilised when learning to read and, in later years, to revise for exams. Visualization of pages of notes, mind mapping, and pictorial representations are all proven methods which individuals can use to aid learning. Visualization has been used to help children grasp unusual and abstract concepts and understand more complicated text.

More prosaically, visual imagery in the forms of photos, television programmes, pictures, adverts, and more, surrounds us. With the constant march of technology, it has never been easier to capture moments electronically, and consume content across different platforms and devices. We also live in an age where our exposure to advertising and marketing imagery has never been greater.

*

[Alan] An important aspect to my lack of visual imagery is that I seek out lots of visual images. My brain seems to like as much visual information as I can feed it; it's probably coping and compensating for not having access to any mental imaginary created by my own mind.

When I was a child I used to read comics, they were really my equivalent of reading books.

When I watched television, I would try to watch numerous programmes – across the four channels we had – all at the same time. I remember we had a 'picture in picture' television, once, and I used to like watching two programs at the same time. Even today, I am always changing channels on the television, almost every few minutes. Yup, I am that bad a television companion!

Pictures and video have become my memories. I try to record as many videos as I possibly can of people, things, just about everything around me. Especially our cat. This is almost a daily thing for me now. Millie (our cat) is not sure of the attention I give her in trying to take the perfect picture/video, but she usually deliverers the killer pose making me laugh.

Images from video/pictures can have the ability to take me back to the moment; not so much as an instant recall thing, more that they provide a form of reminder (emotional and mental) from what happened at that time, so I can at least remember bits of that moment.

Films/television are strangely anomalous for me; I can remember spoken quotes from films or television programs, possibly not the exact wording or phrase but certainly enough detail for me to say the words out loud.

My family and friends all think I take too many videos/pictures, but I think it's an essential part of my condition. It's almost like the visual diary your mind does not have, so the more you take – the more you have the opportunity to remember, and the more complete my history feels.

Television (especially watching movies) is relaxing for me. I guess it is because my mind concentrates so hard on the visual imagery on the screen that my mind is not thinking of doing anything else. For me, TV becomes an immersive experience rather than a purely visual one.

*

Alan's yearning to seek out imagery, to document his life, is something that is shared by a number of contributors.

[MU] Yes, I absolutely crave it. I take photos all the time and look at them.

[SB] Yes. It really depends what it is, but if it's something you can take a photo of, then I do this and look at it.

[RW] Yes! My husband is one of those "Let's live in the moment" people and Aphantasia explains this difference to me so well. He is trying to form a nice visual memory for the future, and I'm trying to capture it the only way I know how!

[AK] I like looking at visual images a lot. I look at a lot of images on my computer and in books.

[TM] Sometimes I do. My dad died almost 10 years ago and I wish I could easily picture his face. I mostly wish for visual imagery when I'm missing something. I satisfy the longing by finding pictures of the people or places. If that doesn't work, then I start writing. I tend to use writing, especially poetry, as my visual imagery.

[AR] Yes, I haven't really found any way that is able to satisfy it though.

[PA] Yes. I watch images and films a lot. It is part of my profession.

[JA] I do. Sometimes, I want to sleep just so I can dream.

[MB2] Visual images are still something I appreciate quite a bit. I like watching media – films, music videos, looking at photos, etc.

[CS2] Yearning might not be the right word for it, but I do like visual arts. I paint and I draw, but can only do that based on an image that already exists – like I paint and draw copying from photographs.

[ML] I can't 'long' for something I have never had. It does annoy me that I am lacking this, and I fill the gaps with words.

[PW] Not really – just never missed it.

[MR2] No. I don't miss what I've never had, but I do wish I had the ability to visualize.

[AY] Not at all. You can't miss something you've never had.

[MH] No, I've grown accustomed to not having any images running through my head.

[DS] Yearning… no. It would be nice, but I don't dwell on it. That seems pointless.

[Anonymous] Not particularly. I never had many posters or pictures on my walls/side tables until I moved to the other side of the world and was homesick, so I printed out around 150 photos and stuck them to my wall in a photo-mosaic pattern. I've kept the same photos with me since then and always put them up on my wall, and I enjoy looking at them but probably wouldn't have many pictures on my wall if I'd stayed in the same country.

[SC] No, I don't long for it. I've never experienced it, even a little, so I don't know what I'm missing out on. Kind of the same with alcohol; I'm way over the legal drinking age, but I've never drunk alcohol. I don't know what I'm missing, so I don't desire it. (I can't drink because of my history with amnesia, drinking apparently might set it off again, and that's a risk I'm never taking.)

[KB] No, I don't yearn for them. I am curious about what the experience might be like, the same way people who are able to visualize are curious about what it must be like not to visualize.

[MR] I wish I could visually remember the important times with my family. The births of my children, their childhood, their marriages, the family gatherings, etc. I have my camera and my diary and can recall the times but the only visual memories I have are captured on film.

[MC] I don't find myself yearning for visual images. Occasionally I feel sad that I lack them, but I also think that at this point in my life it would be overwhelming to have visualization.

[JK] I do wish I could experience visual images but I know there's nothing I can do about it so I don't try to satisfy any longing.

[CS] Well I do now that I know that everyone else can visualize! I can't even imagine it. I would give anything to see what others see. How can this be satisfied?

[TS] Oh I certainly wished I could visualize. Mostly because the lack of [images] means that even the most beautiful sight I've seen is nearly pointless the moment I walk away. Sure, I can take a photo or a video but it still won't capture the smell or touch.

[AT] I think I love the dark and blankness of my mind. It's really very peaceful. I'd like to be able to do things like imagining loved ones' faces though.

*

Alan takes many photos on his phone for, as he explains, "Pictures and video have become my memories. I try to record as many videos as I possibly can of people, things, just about everything around me." Contributors were asked whether they also take lots of photographs.

[TS] Yes, and if it was socially acceptable I'd take a live video feed all the time. It's the only way for me to remember something visually.

[AT] I'm fairly sure I have taken at least one photo a day for as long as I've had a camera on my phone. I need to record and document what we've been up to – everything from tourist attractions, to a photo of a hotel room door so I can find my way back!

[L] This is an understatement! I have over 4,000 pictures on my phone!

[TM] Yes! Many. I love having things to look back at.

[SR] After I understood I'm an Aphant, I started taking lots of pictures to help remember the look of loved ones, places, happenings.

[MR] I have always taken many photos. I never go anywhere without my camera. I also use Google images for places and events I remember but cannot visualize.

[CS] Millions, I don't want to forget my life.

[CH] Yes. Photography is a hobby of mine. I don't do many selfies.

[SC] Yes, I have thousands of photos of sunrises and sunsets; because of where I live, and the work I do, I see almost every one. I also take pictures of most animals I see, so I can show others what snakes/ lizards I found that day.

[SB] Yes. I like having a visual "memory" of things.

[RH] I take some pictures… but not usually for social reasons. I tend to take pictures for reference reasons. Before solid GPS that integrated with technology that knew you had driven somewhere and parked… I would take photos in parking garages and parking lots to remember where I parked. Picture of the cross street located closest to the lot if I was in an unfamiliar city. I take pictures of furniture, or cabinets or fixtures in stores. I take pictures of arrangements on display at stores.

[PW] No, I take fewer than most. I tend to only focus on one thing at a time, so if I focus on taking a picture than I can't focus on the event, and I feel like I end up missing more of the experience. I do, at times, enjoy looking back at pictures though; both those I took and those my loved ones took.

[MC] No, surprisingly I don't take lots of pictures. The ones I have, though, I put up around the house so they're readily accessible.

[AS2] No, but I do continuously look up things on Google 'images', e.g., when I read the book The Goldfinch, I looked up the Goldfinch painting that it referred to and kept looking at it regularly. This enabled me to visualize it as I was reading about it in the book. Likewise, it makes a huge difference if a book has pictures inside it.

[JL] I used to, but only when I wanted to remember something. I have a lot of pictures from holidays, more than people usually take, but I don't consider everyday importance to be memorized. I sometimes take photos of things I like (like a car I like and which I saw on the street), but not for sharing it with others, just for myself.

*

The images that Alan captures take him back to the moment. A number of contributors feel the same.

[MR] Yes, most of the time. They make me laugh or smile or even cry so, yes, I guess they do.

[SB] Yes. Again, they don't really form images in my head but I can remember the things said, the feelings I had, etc.

[JT] They take me back to how something felt, less so to the location.

[LH] I remember the moment but as an event which I have knowledge about; like a story without pictures.

[JL] yes, and it's also connected to keepsakes (souvenirs, mementos – little things that remind me of the moments).

[DG] Very much so. Not a great detail of the event, but moments, yes.

[RW] Not usually, I don't think. But I may recall some things about that moment, and those things can make me feel the fitting emotions.

[MU] They do not – not at all.

[MC] No. They remind me that an event happened, but I do not re-experience anything (sights, sounds, emotions) from the moment.

[JA] Not sure it takes me back to any moment. I feel emotions when I look at images.

[CS] I can remember bits and pieces that happen. I can't go back to the moment; that literally makes no sense to me.

*

Television is a medium that is central to modern life and which some people cannot get enough of. Channel surfing, box set bingeing, and the plethora of channels for all interests – television feeds many people's needs. Indeed, Alan's enjoyment of television is commonly shared.

[RW] Yes. In particular, I LOVE watching a show or a movie of a book I've read! One of my biggest joys of TV actually. Also, having an enticing story is much more important to me in a movie than strong visuals, since it's only the story that I get to take away with me.

[MR2] Yes, as long as it doesn't jump around a lot between characters or time periods. I sometimes have difficulty following shows like that and lose interest in them.

[ST] Yes, if it is interesting.

[CW] Yes, but I often multitask several shows, a tablet, and other tasks.

[PA] Yes, if it is very good show. I can watch two or three screens at the same time.

[SR] I love to watch several episodes in a row.

[ML] Yes, it keeps me entertained. I have it in every room, and watch while doing other things, like […] cooking, or ironing, or talking on the telephone. I never just watch the TV, it is just an 'extra' to stop me getting bored.

[PW] Yes, but not as much as many. I can't watch too much at a time unless I'm doing other things at the same time, and then the TV is really background noise since I can't do multiple things well.

[JT] Yes, but I don't remember them very long unless they strike me emotionally. I am very good at giving a concise description of a movie, while I've noticed other people tend to go on and on with details that seem unnecessary to me.

[TS] I don't watch a lot of TV these days but whether it's related to Aphantasia I do not know.

[SB] No, not really.

[Anonymous] Nope. But that has more to do with the general content on television. I haven't watched television for eight years or so now. I do sometimes watch series or movies though – which I can really enjoy.

[JL] I have trouble, unless I'm watching with someone. I like watching movies in cinema, as there is nothing to distract me.

[AT] I hate television! I find fictional programming so dull – I don't feel like it enhances my life in any way. I much prefer listening to a podcast that might broaden my knowledge, or put a documentary on the telly in the background.

Chapter 6: Sleeping and Dreaming

We all sleep, but do we all dream?

Dreams can be defined as a series of thoughts, images, feelings, and ideas, experienced in the mind during sleep, which occur involuntarily. There is currently no scientific consensus on the exact purpose behind dreaming, although the study of dreams – oneirology – has progressed significantly since the discovery of sleep phases in the 1950s.

While dreams can vary quite significantly, both in terms of content and the way in which the dream is actually experienced by each person, there are also many shared traits.

The vast majority of dreams are forgotten either immediately, or very quickly after waking. Research suggests the ability to recall dreams can be influenced by various additional factors, including avoiding delays in waking up and having a desire to recall them. People are also more likely to remember emotionally distressing dreams.

The most common themes identified in dreams include falling, flying, being unable to find a toilet, and failing exams. However, while many dreams adhere to common themes, there can also be significant variation in our experience of dreaming.

Most people dream from a first-person perspective, yet some report dreaming from a third-person perspective, meaning they see themselves in their dreams. Others dream that they are somebody else entirely. Moreover, while most people dream in colour, it is estimated that around 12 percent dream in black and white.

The 'purpose' behind dreams has been the subject of considerable debate for centuries. Sigmund Freud, for instance, famously hypothesized that dreaming was the unconscious expression of forbidden desires, anxieties, or wishes. Although no consensus exists to this day, advances in neuroscience have helped to improve our understanding.

A 2011 study provides scientific support for the idea that dreams have a key role to play in processing emotions, while further research has suggested dreams also help with consolidating memories and newly-learned information. This would appear to indicate that dreams serve to assist with knowledge retention.

According to some studies, somewhere in the region of 70 percent of all dreams include a threatening situation. This has led to the development of a 'threat simulation hypothesis' which suggests dreams play a role in preparing us for tackling danger, serving as a type of simulation or rehearsal for the threats we may face in real life.

*

[Alan] I dream when I'm asleep, and I sometimes 'remember the dream'. My ability to remember is very short-term; if I do not remember it within minutes of waking up, I will not remember anything.

When I recall my dream, I see lots of visual imaginary. I can only remember what has happened in dreams for the first 30 minutes of being awake, mostly for nightmares I think; I don't remember as many of the good or nice dreams, mainly the bad ones. It could be that the bad ones are simply more vivid with stronger emotions to remember and recall when I wake up.

I recently found out (while writing this book) that I dream in colour; until then I was not sure if I did or did not. It was thanks to a weird dream where I dreamt about a duck; I saw the greens and browns in the darkness.

My ability to dream makes no sense to me at all and is possibly why it's difficult for others to comprehend my condition, because I find it totally perplexing as well.

When I am asleep I can visualize and see images in my mind, but as soon as my eyelids are opened and I am awake the images in my mind disappear and I see nothing. It's as if I have a mental switch that shuts down the images in my mind as soon as I am awake or my eyes are closed.

I have the ability to daydream but not with any visual detail.

As mentioned, I am more likely to remember nightmares than usual dreams. My frequency of nightmares does appear to be linked to my personal stress levels; the more stress I feel, the more likely I am to have a nightmare. As a child, I think I had some influence over the content or story of my dreams.

I think that if I did not dream whilst asleep, I would have discovered my lack of mental imagery sooner. Surely, I would have questioned my ability to dream with images while asleep but not when I close my eyes?

Also, when I dream, I see objects and things which do not exist in the real world, so I know I have created them in my mind! I know this because I have dreamt about spaceships and weapons that I have not seen in any film, and I have also seen people in my dreams that I would never have met in real life, alongside buildings and architecture that don't exist.

The details of these things elude me. I can sense they were in my dream but I cannot describe or explain them in any depth afterwards. It's like knowing you are looking at a 10-storey building but only getting the detail a child may draw; the things I see up close, during the dream, are in the correct detail and in focus. This further adds to the puzzle and my confusion of the condition.

I feel like sleeping is the least affected part of Aphantasia as a whole. It seems closest to what people without the condition experience.

I remember very little from any dreams after the short term, but I am often left with a mental impression, especially if they have been very vivid. I look back now at the times when I was told to think of sheep when trying to drop off to sleep. I never really understood it when my parents told me, I just assumed it was a figure of speech and not representative of real life.

Does everyone dream? I know someone with Aphantasia who has no dreams at all.

Daydreaming is a particularly strange thing for me as it involves no images. How do I dream when asleep and apparently lucidly but not when awake? I don't think of shapes or objects when daydreaming, I think of scenario-based problems to solve. I have developed and improved this ability over the years and can daydream quite easily given the right conditions.

*

Do you dream when you are asleep?

[MB] No.

[ST] No.

[MC] I dream in blackness, with some spatial awareness. The little I understand of what's going on is only because my own mind is making the dream up. As a child, I rationalized it as my dreams were taking place behind me where I couldn't see. Or hear.

[PA] Yes. Sometimes very vividly with details like movies.

[AS] So, when I dream, I can see things. But they're never super vivid or even very clear. They always seem like they're on the verge of being real, imagery-wise. The feelings and experiences in my dreams feel real while I'm dreaming, even if the images are fuzzy.

[JS] Yes I have no problem dreaming but, like memories, cannot recall them apart from basic descriptive facts. One of the strangest experiences is being able to have some form of involuntary images appear in the "twilight" moment before I fall asleep. It is usually associated with whatever train of thought I was following before I reached that point. Any realisation of the fact that I'm not asleep yet and the images slip away instantly.

[RW] Yes, very vividly. And my dreams actually use all of my senses.

[TM] Oh yes. Very, very vividly. I've had reoccurring nightmares since I was a kid. I am also prone to night terrors. While the night terrors disappear right after I have them, they tend to be of the same sort. Mostly snakes falling from my ceiling.

[AT] Sort of, maybe. I definitely have times where I wake up with a story in my head, but there's no dreaming in the traditional sense of the word. I don't have images to match the narrative.

[AY] Very often. Very lucidly. I know that I'm dreaming.

[JA] Yes, vivid colour. Even during naps.

[DS] Yes, I have very vivid dreams. All my senses work in my dreams.

[JK2] Frequently, sometimes recurring, and sometimes I have lucid dreams where I am in control. The best are recurring lucid dreams that I can try to change from a nightmare into something better each time I have them.

[JL] Very, very rarely. In the past year, it happened five times, and two of them were just nightmares from sleep paralysis; the other three were induced by strong emotion. In all of these cases, the dreams were broken by waking up.

[L] I have magnificent dreams. Sometimes they are like lucid dreaming, such that I am really in the dream. Sometimes I remember dreams, sometimes I do not. Sometimes I have dreams that make me feel wonderful when I wake up, especially dreams where I can fly. Some dreams are nonsensical and others seem to be profound. I cannot close my eyes and revisit a dream but I can think about them and contemplate.

[Anonymous] Not often, and if I do I only remember the dream in words (I can't remember if I have ever had a visual dream).

[PW] Until recently I would have insisted no – that I do not and never have dreamed. The more I learn about how Aphantasia affects me though, beyond just not seeing images, the more I've started to have the occasional 'dream'. I can't recall anything later, and I'm pretty sure they weren't images, but I do know now that I dream in some sense occasionally. But it still seems to be very rare.

I don't think I dream in images. I don't recall any nightmares since I don't recall any dreams. I do, however, have a belief that I had a "fuzzy feeling" that was unpleasant at times during sleep, much like I assume a nightmare would be.

*

Do you dream in colour?

[MH] No.

[JK2] No. If an object is specifically associated with a colour (oceans are blue) then I "know" that the black and white ocean in my dream is "actually" blue, but that's it.

[MR2] I believe I do somewhat. Not vivid colours, but muted colours like technicolour.

[AY] Full colour and sound. It's as vivid as real life.

[KB] I have had two nightmares in my entire life that I remember, and woke up from and both were like watching a colour movie.

[SC] Yes, all my dreams are in vivid colour, I've only dreamed in black and white once, and that was a challenge.

*

How long can you remember your dreams for?

[AY] A few seconds after I wake up, they fade. Nothing I do can make me remember them. I've tried.

[CS2] There are only two dreams that I still remember today which were very vivid and scary. Usually, I forget the rare dreams I have by the time I get up from bed.

[CS] Until I wake up. I know I have dreamt vividly but as soon as I wake it's gone. Very rarely I will remember something I dreamt about.

[ML] Usually just a few moments, but more dramatic ones can stay for longer. I once dreamt that I had been to work and did overtime too. When I woke, I was furious because I had to go to work and do it all again. The outline of that one stays with me to this day!

[TS] Most dreams I forget the instant I wake up. Some fade out during the following day. Some special few were important enough that they turn into a memory story so I'll always remember them.

[DS] Most of the time I don't remember them, or they are gone soon after I wake up. I've had a handful of lucid dreams (the subject has always fascinated me), and those are much easier to remember once I wake up.

[JR] Depends. It can stay with me for hours or even all day if there's an emotion attached to it. If I'm very happy or sad when I wake up, usually the happy feelings stay with me longer. I can feel a positive emotion an entire day sometimes, even without thinking about the dream itself. Also, if I describe it to someone or even just to myself, the memory including details sticks a little longer.

[CS2] Nightmares definitely stay longer. I will sometimes remember dreams that make me upset (like my husband asking for a divorce) for a little after I wake up, but the details of the dream fade away within seconds and I'm left with the gist of the story and an overwhelming sad feeling.

[JT] Scared is an emotion, so nightmares are more memorable. I did have an interesting experience recently regarding nightmares after learning about Aphantasia. I woke up from a nightmare and was afraid to go back to sleep. I was thinking about how much worse it would be if I could visualize, and closed my eyes just to ensure I wouldn't "see" the monster from my dream, and of course, I couldn't. Then, I changed the story, just by telling myself the dream wasn't real, and then the emotion of being scared immediately went away, and I went right back to sleep!

[KB] I don't often remember my dreams. Most of the dreams I do remember are like the same thinking style as when I am awake, apart from the fact that people turn into dogs, and houses into buses!

[MB2] [I remember dreams] sometimes for quite a long time, but as concepts. For example, I still remember a dream I had several years ago that [involved] a cement mixer. I can't visually remember this dream (or any others), but I remember the "plot points" of each dream fairly well.

*

As detailed above, Alan daydreams. His daydreams tend to revolve around problem-solving. No visual images are involved.

[KB] I used to daydream lots as a child. Not so much now that I practice mindfulness. Never with imagery; I never see images in my mind. I simply think the daydream and it evokes emotions.

[ND] I daydream; there are no images associated with it. I can think of being in a place and what I would feel like being there, or I can daydream in a more imaginary sense and create narratives in my head.

[Anonymous] It is difficult to know how to class 'daydreaming'. I always think of a cover of "What Katy Did at School" (Puffin Classics) where (in my expression-body language/spatial memory) Katy is looking bored and staring out the window. Note this is not a visual memory. I've just Googled the actual cover, and found she's actually staring at the viewer.

In any case, if you class daydreaming as thinking about things unrelated to what's happening in your present situation, and also being not particularly immediately useful, I daydream a lot.

It seems to be a mix of not-quite-complete inner voice sentences, feelings, expression-body-language/spatial/sound memories or imaginings of past, future or fictional situations, songs… It's basically me getting distracted and going off on a long chain of domino thoughts.

Sometimes I can guide it, and I think it would be really useful if I could actually make myself daydream about work projects, but mostly it doesn't work that way. I walk a lot, and I don't listen to music while I walk because I prefer daydreaming.

[MR2] I replay things in my head, but it's more like having an ongoing conversation with myself.

[AR] My mind sometimes wanders, in that I start thinking about random things; however, it involves no imagery and is purely a train of thought.

[RH] Yes I daydream, but no imagery. It's mostly around what I would rather be doing or feeling in that moment.

[SC] Yes, but it is never accompanied by imagery. I'll often be doing nothing and I'll just start thinking of random things, and totally zone out of the real world.

[CH] I tell stories to myself, often when bored driving home from work. "What if xxx happened, what would I or others do?" or "How cool would it be if xxx happened, and consequences." etc.

[MB2] I do daydream, but it isn't very visual. I will often think at length about scenarios – e.g., a party I am going to have, food I will eat later – but these daydreams are dim and brief in their imagery. They are more like imagined emotions or pleasant ideas.

I often daydream of being rich, but I don't daydream about things I will do if I am ever rich – my daydreams about this are exclusively just feelings that might be related to the daydream, or that I imagine would be associated with images if I could visually daydream. For example, when I daydream of being rich, I often think along the lines of "Wow, things would be much more relaxing and less stressful if I was rich" rather than what I think someone with imaging capabilities would daydream about when they fantasize about being rich, like drinking fancy wine and expensive cheese on the balcony of their fancy rich house.

[CS2] When I'm daydreaming, it's almost like I'm one of the people in Plato's cave allegory. I can see vague shapes and shadows (only sometimes, and for a fraction of a second only) – I know there is a "real world" outside the cave, but I can't see it.

It's hard to explain, but I daydream in abstract ideas. I can bring up the idea of a cat in my head, without having to see the cat or even verbalize it as 'cat'. It's just there as an idea. The same goes for actions and more complex thoughts.

[DG] I don't daydream.

[JA] No. I ponder things, but I can't daydream in an imaginary way. No visuals at all.

[JK2] I've always understood "daydreaming" to be using my imagination during the daytime, not a separate process. I create an invisible "set" in the blackness of my mind, complete with invisible actors. I then use words and concepts to bring it to life.

Words come strapped with all kinds of baggage – and it's not all visual. So my invisible set might be in a "seedy nightclub" complete with all of the feelings, sounds, and smells (that I neither smell nor hear, but know would be there) that come with those two words. I then use words to make the scene play out. "Stan leaps over the second-storey railing, dropping heavily to the first floor and knocking over a chair as he staggers forward..." while mentally moving the invisible "Stan" character from point A to B.

It's hard to describe but works just fine for me. This is also how books play out in my head.

[JK] Yeah, I daydream. But I usually play scenarios in my head, without anything visual.

[JR] My daydreams do not contain imagery. I may think about something I saw or read or a conversation I had, but that's it. I think about them. Or sometimes ruminate!

[JT] I daydream about things that might happen, or how I wished things could have happened. No visualization. How things might feel.

[MR] [Daydreaming] is nearly always a verbal commentary.

*

When dreaming, are you able to see things that your mind must have created? Things that do not exist in your world at all?

[Anonymous] Yes. I dream visually, and of fantastical things as well as mundane things.

[JA] Yes, all of the time in great amazing detail.

[BM] I see images while I am dreaming, and those images can be of things that do not exist in the real world. I can also sometimes catch mental images if I am just falling asleep, starting to dream, and am jolted awake. However, those images fade very quickly.

[SC] Yes, all the time, I often create things myself, and also see out of this world things. I've flown at thousands of times faster than the speed of light, and far beyond the observed universe.

[AR] No, everything that I see is something I have seen before, although it may behave in abnormal ways, such as objects being able to fly. But most dreams are fairly realistic in their content.

[MR2] No.

[VD] No, I pretty much see things I've seen before; modified things (bigger, different shape/contours).

[AY] Not at all.

[PA] No. Never.

[ML] No, I don't think so. It is mostly everyday things.

[TM] My dreams are almost always realistic. I rarely have fantastical dreams. Maybe that is what makes them scarier.

[GD] I think so. But I really don't know. Do floating, world-dominating puppets count?

[CS2] Mostly they are things that exist in the world – I think (it's hard to be sure when I can't remember my dreams and I don't have many of them to poll from in the first place). [I still remember one dream from] when I was seven; it was particularly vivid and involved killer man-eating Christmas trees, so I guess it was a modified version of something that does exist in the real world.

[LH] My dreams are very vivid. I sometimes dream of things that I've never actually seen; usually, I dream more familiar things but just exaggerated.

[JK2] I think everything, even spaceships, comes from something we've seen in our world. If someone saw an episode of any space-science fiction film, then they've seen spaceships and their mind can recall those images. In that case, I don't think so. But, I did dream about shooting a Tyrannosaurus Rex with a rocket launcher, and dropping fireballs on a horde of zombies, and I've only ever seen either of those on television.

[TS] I can't see things well enough in my head to analyse whether they're completely new or something I've actually seen somewhere.

Chapter 7: Memories

The human brain has two main memory sections: long-term and short-term memory.

Short-term memory usually holds only a few items at a time. For example, when you remember a sequence of numbers – perhaps a code – and yet it can be forgotten moments later. Long-term memory holds more permanent memories. The more you retrieve a memory, the more likely it is to turn into a long-term memory. This is because the retrieval process 're-fires' the transmissions between neurons to create lasting changes in their molecular structures. Through this, memories become hard-wired into our brains.

The Prefrontal Cortex, which is part of the brain's Frontal Lobe, is the region responsible for short-term memory. The task of consolidating short-term memories into long-term memories is performed by the Hippocampus, which is located in the brain's Temporal Lobe. After the memory is consolidated, it is stored in the Cerebral Cortex. This is the area of the brain responsible for long-term memory.

*

[Alan] Memories have always been difficult for me. I struggle to remember almost anything with any detail, and usually cover my abilities with the jokey comment, *"My memory is just like Swiss cheese. It's full of holes."*

Saying that, I do remember some things from my life, but I cannot decide or define the level of detail for any memories, it just does not seem to work that way. It almost feels predetermined and more like random, to be honest.

Having three or four seconds of a two-hour movie is probably the total amount of time I remember for my whole childhood. I know of past events in my life but these are very limited, and I tend not to rely on my knowledge or historical memory. I have no actual images in my mind, only memories that are created from looking at pictures.

But I know things have happened in my past. I have knowledge of them even though there is no manifestation of an image. Even with the sureness of knowing it happened, I do wonder with some past events whether I dreamed them.

Additionally, I struggle with the concept of relative time. I cannot determine when an event occurred in my life compared to another. It's like a fact you know to be true but to which you have no proof to show others.

While writing this book, I looked at some of the pictures from my childhood. I have no original memories other than the recollections and emotions triggered from viewing the pictures themselves, and no ability to retrieve any imagery or memories that I would consider first-hand. I am never able to see the memory through my own eyes.

Also, I can't remember a time when I can recall having any form of visual imagery; I have no memories of childhood that are not triggered by me viewing a picture from these times.

Some smells, and textures, are logged as memories in my mind; when I smell or touch, I can re-activate that past event in some way, as feelings and emotions linked to the past. I have asked fellow sufferers and they confirm that their other senses are often impacted by Aphantasia.

Memories, for me, appear to be connected. For example, if I can remember one thing, I am able to remember events or things linked to, or triggered by, thinking about that event. This daisy-chaining of thoughts is kind of random, though, as I have no control of which past events appear as memories, or the level of detail that can be retrieved. Also, I cannot access other memories further along my memory line without that original memory; I could not simply jump straight to other individual thoughts.

*

In the survey for this book, contributors were asked to rate their memory and determine whether Aphantasia has an effect.

[KB] My memory is okay.

[MB] I have a good memory for facts, not for people.

[Anonymous] I think I have a very good memory. The Aphantasia only affects the way my memories are stored: in words, rather than in visuals/sounds/smells/tastes.

[JL] I have quite a good memory, better than most people; it includes very good memories of what people said in talks with me or situations. I have a bad memory for details from other sources (colours, weather, surroundings).

[JR] My general memory is fine. I am really good at all sorts of trivia. I remember how to play complicated card games. I don't remember things like people's cars, even those of people close to me except I know that my son's is white and my sister has two cars that are different shades of blue. I've walked to what I thought were friends' cars thinking they were the right ones. Oops.

Guys didn't have to worry about impressing me with their cars – not only am I not into material things, I'd have no clue what they were driving.

It takes me a long time to notice a change in buildings I pass by regularly, such as if they've been painted or replaced by a different business and things like that.

I do have an excellent memory for numbers, (I've memorized my driver's license #, my library card # (14 digits), my credit card #, etc.). I am a savant at remembering birthdays; I even remember some birthdays of people I may not have seen in decades. I remember song lyrics. Once I know them, I don't forget them.

[CW] I have a better than normal memory.

[PW] I have a very good memory for facts – a great memory for things I read that I am interested in.

[CS] My memory is pretty good.

I don't remember memories, faces, sequences, or specific details very well. I remember facts; my sense of direction is good. I could tell you what my school looked like when I was seven, and how to get around it. I know what's on a road but I can't visualize it. I just know it.

[CH] My memory is weird. I can't remember movies I've watched very well if they were mediocre/not my favourites. Upon rewatching, I'll know I've seen it, but often it takes a third time through, to remember the ending. Favourite movies, movies that I've seen many times, movies that made an impression on me – I remember fine.

[TS] I can remember things as a list of facts. Feelings get turned into words and memorized like that. I can remember very little before starting school. After that, I remember a bunch of individual events. I have no idea if I remember more of them than most people do.

[CS2] My memory is almost inexistent. It's ridiculously bad, to the point it's almost comical.

I don't remember things from the past very well, I can't remember tasks I have to do, and I can't remember important conversations. Some memories do stick with me though – some negative ones might stick around longer.

When I was getting tested for ADHD, they did a functional memory test as well, and I scored ridiculously low on that – the psychiatrist was quite surprised to see a score so low. Looking back on it now, knowing about Aphantasia, I think it does affect my memory. On one of the tests, he would tell me a short story of five or six sentences long, and I would recall the story in as much detail as I could right afterwards. It makes sense now that if I'm not creating a mental image of the story – the fact that the girl was wearing a pink shirt and not a yellow one – it doesn't really stay with me.

[ML] My memory is pants. I live life via lists and calendars. However, I believe my subconscious is brilliant at it. I'll be doing something and realize that I used a possibly incorrect postcode, or similar, on a document hours ago. I get a chance to put things right that way. It is an itch at the back of my mind, and then it surfaces.

[MB2] I don't have a good working memory, and I definitely think Aphantasia affects my memory. I have a hard time remembering my day to day activities, what words others say to me, or what my schedule is like in the future. I keep a meticulous day planner because I am often very anxious that I am forgetting to do something important. I have a Generalized Anxiety Disorder, and I think my lack of memory is what makes me anxious a lot of the time.

[ND] Aphantasia affects my ability to have a literal image of memories but I know where I was, who was there, and in some cases, what they were wearing.

[MU] My memory is appallingly terrible, and I think it has gotten worse over time.

[AR] I'd say I have fairly poor short-term memory, although my long-term memory is relatively good.

[LH] My memory for words is dreadful. I can remember places from my childhood but cannot see them in my head though I could describe them to a basic level. I'm good at remembering numbers if I repeat them a few times.

[L] Aphantasia definitely affects my memory. This is "part" of the GIFT that is my blackness. I can easily move on, forget, not hold grudges, no living in the past, and no dreaming of the future. This is it! I can live in the NOW.

[MH] My memory is horrendous. There is a process in memorization that requires a call back of which I have none. Now, truth be told, not a day goes by when I don't try to use the process of 'call back' but 99% of the time, nothing but blankness is 'called back'.

[MR2] I am terrible at remembering people's names and anything that requires memorization. I believe this is 100% due to Aphantasia.

[JT] I have been told I 'remember things wrong'. My details of events are limited. I remember how I felt, and then I remember the things that happened that support how I felt, which means I leave out a lot of things that didn't support my feelings/perspective. I don't think all of my memories are "accurate"…

[JS] My memory is very factually-based, with recollection popping into my head. I've been told at work that I've got a very good memory, but this is usually for things that happened within the last week.

[JA] I have a terrible memory. I forget so many things, from events to where I left my phone.

*

An inability to recall people's faces is frequently cited by contributors as one of the negatives of Aphantasia, although issues surrounding recognition seem less problematic or common.

[RW] I can't recall faces in my mind, but after I've seen someone, I can definitely identify them from a line-up. I can also describe faces to you in terms of prominent qualities, but I couldn't answer questions such as "what's the approximate distance between her eyes?" or answer questions about details that I didn't find notable ("What is his chin like?").

[MR] I cannot recall people's faces. The only 'memories' I have of what my parents, friends, and relations look like is from photos. I have trouble remembering any event that is not recorded in physical form.

[LH] If a close friend or family member passes me I would recognize them, but if you asked me to describe my daughter I would tell you facts like she has a mole on her arm, she wears glasses, and she has long blonde hair. I know these as facts but cannot describe them in any detail. If my neighbour walked past me in the supermarket, I would not recognize her. If I see people out of context, I rarely recognize who they are.

[JR] [Remembering faces] In person, yes, very well. In fact, although I may not remember where or when I met someone, I recognize them even after not seeing them for a while.

I am good at seeing family resemblances. Also, I don't know if this is related to Aphantasia, but I'll often say so-and-so looks like someone I know, e.g., Matthew McConaughey reminds me of my brother. I don't know if it's because I'm being perceptive or if it's just 'a touch' of face blindness – seeing very broad similarities. Specifically, in regards to face blindness, I never thought I had it, but I realized lately that it has come up when I'm watching a TV movie; if there are two actresses who are similar in age and hair colour/length, I may confuse them for a few scenes. This never happens with people I've met in person though.

[RH] I cannot see faces in my mind, but I remember traits. I recognize people when I see them, but I sometimes struggle when I see someone that I don't know well out of a normal context. They will look "familiar" to me, but I won't be able to place where I know them from.

[MR] I cannot remember faces as in, I cannot visualize them and could not describe them; BUT if I see someone I know, I know who they are. People are often bemused by the fact that I can work with someone or know someone for years and not be able to confirm that they have a beard or wear glasses. Sometimes, I notice if they have changed something about their appearance but I am not sure what.

[JK2] I can't visually recall details of what a person looks like, but when I see the person, I have no problem associating my memories of that person to who I am looking at. It takes me several meetings to get familiar with someone's face and if I've only seen a person a few times I can easily mistake them for someone else with similar features. It's not like I have to re-introduce myself to people every time I meet them!

[MB2] I'm terrible at remembering faces. I do this thing where I can meet someone three or four times and they'll tell me we've met before, and I'll feign recognition until they tell me their name, at which point I can remember everything they've ever said to me – that information is tied to their name in my mind, not their face.

[AS2] I have a terrible memory for faces, especially if I see someone out of context or if they've changed something about themselves, e.g., their hair, etc. I do remember people very close to me and/or who I see very regularly. Strangely, I remember EVERY person from my class at primary school, and some from my secondary school, so I don't believe that I've had this condition all my life.

110

[MR2] Yes, I recognize them, but I can't describe them. I have great difficulty remembering names. When I'm introduced to someone, I can ask them their name half a dozen different times in the same conversation and not remember their name five minutes later; but I will remember that we met. If I haven't seen someone for a while (other than close family members or close friends), I won't remember who they are. They may look vaguely familiar, but I can't place them.

[CS] I remember faces, but I don't know who they are. I can't put names to them. I couldn't picture a person if their name was said, either; they would have to be standing in front of me to know. I could barely describe my own children.

[BM] I am very good at recognizing faces, but I am not good at recalling and describing the details of faces.

[SB] I'm really bad at remembering faces and I've struggled with it my whole life. I mostly can only recognize people who I saw a couple of times before.

[Anonymous] After much thought, I've come to the conclusion that I don't really remember faces, I remember expressions/body language. I recognize people through a general idea that they (for example) have short black hair, are tall, plus their usual set of facial expressions and/or the way they move. I have a non-visual working memory for facial expressions/body language – I can hold them in my mind for a while, whereas I have no visual working memory.

I've done some Prosopagnosia tests, and I did better than I expected on some of them, I think because you had to choose a face that was the same as a previous face, and I just chose *the one with the same expression*. I'm not good at recognizing some actors – if they change their set of body language/expressions for a film, I'm a bit lost. I'm also not good with acquaintances – I need to interact with them enough to build up a set of expressions to recognize them by.

[TS] I can recognize [faces] later on relatively well. I can't bring them up in my head at all. Or describe them.

[ND] I am very good with faces, but I don't always remember the name associated with the face.

[ST] The majority of the time, yes [I can remember faces] however not always when out of context.

[SR] [I cannot remember faces] though I recognize them very well.

[Anonymous] If I spend enough time with someone I will store enough data about how that person looks so I can recognize that person the next time I see him/her.

[L] I know people when I see them. I use the term re-cognize, but I do not see them, I just know them. Many people that I approach that I know don't remember me, but after the connection they do.

[JT] I can't recall faces as images in my head if not looking at them or a picture, but once I see someone again, I can place them. I don't always recognize people I've only met once.

[JS] I am good at remembering faces but poor at remembering names. If the face is not in front of me, then I cannot picture it or remember details past hair colour and length.

[AY] Yes. But I often struggle to associate a name to the face or where I know them from. So I'll often know I know someone but not know why.

[AT] I'm pretty crap with faces. I definitely don't have prosopagnosia, but I do have to make a concerted effort to remember people. Usually, I make a 'verbal' note of a distinct feature to help me recall who I'm talking to or where I know them from. After I've met someone a few times, I am fine though.

*

For visualizers, memories are often conjured up through the process of revisiting static and moving images in their minds' eyes. Accordingly, 're-seeing' an event can confirm its occasion and can help to surface relevant details.
Contributors were asked how their memories manifest and how they discern that events took place. Perhaps as feelings...

[MH] It is almost always a feeling... actually, I'd say that it is always a feeling.

[AK] It must be a feeling... I see nothing. It may be associated with thinking about an age, a time, a person, a feeling, a taste, a smell, a place.

[SR] Maybe [a] kind of feeling, yes. I guess the best way to describe it is, that I kind of use words in my mind to be sure of what is happening and what has been going on earlier.

[SB] Yeah, there are feelings but also thoughts and memories. I still can remember things even if I can't see them in my mind's eye – I know what happened, I can recall it, there's just no image. Also, for example, when I remember my classroom, I can tell you what you could see when you looked out of the window because I know it and I saw it. It's just that I can't recreate the picture in my head, but that doesn't mean I don't know what was there.

[MB2] It's a feeling, for sure. But it also just feels like I have a repository of "facts" in my head somewhere that I have a hard time accessing unless prompted (or which are very memorable).

[AS] I wouldn't say it's a feeling exactly, even though it is. I mean, I remember things happening. It's no different than a blind person experiencing life. How do they know things have happened in their lives if they can't see them? They still experience them, same as me. The difference is I saw them as they happened, and can't see them again.

[DS] It's not a feeling. When I recall memories, I am pulling up stored information. Calling it a feeling doesn't come close to what I'm experiencing.

[TS] My memories are a story, like an audiobook told by the voice in my head or a list of facts.

[TM] How do all people know that events have taken place? I just know it. My memories are solid and I often write about them later, which helps. Wouldn't it be true that people with strong visual memories would also have to go on faith that the memory actually happened?

[CS] I know they happened. I think I would forget more if I didn't have photos. I sometimes describe it like being Neo in The Matrix; I don't visualize anything, it is just word. I don't visualize the words either, but that's as close as I can come to describing it. Sometimes I can visualize something, but it is invisible. I know that makes absolutely no sense. I can picture an event, and I can picture what happened in parts, but I never see anything, I just know it. I move through remembering events like you may move through Google Maps Street View; it's like a series of pictures strung together to form a larger picture…

[CH] I remember facts of events: what and where. I will remember emotions of emotional events, like how nervous I was for cheerleading try-outs. I don't know the how.

[ST] It will be a story told or a feeling that I have kept.

[RW] It's mostly knowledge. I think it's like… if you think of something over and over, and you experience the emotions that correlate to those events over and over, you solidify some mental circuits?

[RH] I suspect in the same way a person who was born blind can. It's conversations and feelings.

[PA] It is a story, not an image. I know when it happened, where, who was there, what everyone did and said.

[MU] It is just a sense of trust that they did.

[MR2] It's more like knowing facts. Like how do you know that fire is hot or ice is cold? How do you know that wool is itchy or silk is smooth? How do you know that your bed is soft or the floor is hard? I remember facts about things and even if I was happy or sad, but I can't create a picture in my mind of it, or feel the same emotions that I felt at the time.

[ML] It is a story. A quick-fire retelling. A mental diary.

[MC] I know the facts of an event. Generally, I remember that I may have felt a certain way at the time, but I do not feel the feeling itself.

[L] Experience is not a vision, it is an experience. That experience may have feelings associated with it. Just because there is no vision does not make it immaterial. If I want to create an experience, I think about it, put my thoughts towards it. There is no image. Yeah, people often say, "That's weird, how do you do anything!"

[JT] I utilize others and trust that their recollection of things is accurate. Often I won't remember something until someone else talks about it. If I "did" something, I have a better chance of remembering it, than if I just witnessed something mundane.

I can remember that I drank milk this morning because I can recall the act of pouring milk, but I can't picture the glass of milk. I know I used my favourite mug because it evoked the emotion of love, as it was given to me by my sister. I can tell you it's a purple mug because I have committed those facts to memory, but I can't picture it.

[JK2] How do blind people know events have taken place in their lives if they couldn't visualize them? Life and experience are more than just what we perceive with our eyes. There are sights, sounds, smells, textures, emotions, reactions, motions, and probably more that I am missing. Just because I can't call up a visual, Polaroid photograph memory of what my wedding dress looks like doesn't mean I can't remember and repeat that I got married in a wedding dress or the details of that wedding dress.

[CS2] The earliest memory I have, is not a true memory at all. It's vaguely related to something that happened, but I guess I changed it up enough in my head that it's now totally false. It never happened. I know that because rationally it doesn't make sense. There are no crocodiles in this part of the country, and even if there were, I don't think my uncle would be able to wrestle it – and win.

This is a question I often ask myself. Some things I know they happened because that's what I tell myself happened. How trustworthy is that? If your past experiences make up who you are today, how can I know who I am, if I'm not sure who I was? This is something I struggle with, and I have recently thought of keeping a diary, writing a memoir, or keeping a photo journal to help keep track of my memories.

On the plus side, I sometimes get to experience this for the first time again. Since I forget what I did/what it was like, it's like doing it for the first time.

*

Can you connect memories to emotions?

[GD] YES!! I would say that is my strongest memory system.

[JR] Yes, very much so. I am an emotional person; not detached at all. I'm also very empathetic.

[TS] Sometimes. If how I felt was important to the actual memory I remember the feeling as a fact. 'I remember I felt scared' instead of 'I remember I felt like this'.

[PW] Yes. I don't have many memories possibly, nor do I seem to be emotional, but the things I do remember the most about are tied to strong emotions. I even tend to seek out new/big experiences possibly because they will "stick" more with my memory.

[JA] Absolutely. It's the only way I can connect things.

[JL] Yes, the strongest emotions I remember longest and best.

[MU] Yes, I can do that. I am very emotionally-engaged with my life.

[KB] Yes. For example, some of the earliest memories I remember are of a holiday to New Zealand when I was four. I remember the awe I felt seeing a huge Weta insect shell on a tree. The smell of the hot mud at Rotorua. The joy of swimming in a friend's pool and jumping on the trampoline. The cold of the black pebble beach. The excitement of cooking the potatoes we just dug out of the garden. Feeling safe and loved.

[MR2] Not really. I know that I was happy at my wedding and sad when my friend died, but I don't feel the emotions anymore even when I remember the event.

[MB2] Not really. Past emotions exist as facts in my head – e.g., when this specific event happened, I felt very distraught or sad – but remembering the event itself does not trigger those emotions within me.

[DS] Emotions are one the strongest memory builders. I remember how I felt in the past, but I don't feel that emotion when I am remembering the event.

[BM] Yes, but I do not re-experience those emotions. I simply know that I had them and that they might have affected me in several ways at the time.

*

Alan wrote, "I struggle with the concept of relative time. I cannot determine when an event occurred in my life compared to another." Contributors shared whether they were able to work out relative time effectively.

[AS] Yes, absolutely.

[JL] Yes, I have no problem with that usually.

[PW] Yes, that is not a problem at all. I may not remember many mundane events, or be able to recall them on demand, but I have no problem with relative time between events I do recall in my way.

[SC] Yes, but it is very hard, I have to spend time thinking about it, but even then, if two things happened in the same place, it's very hard for me to tell them apart.

[MC] I can line up events chronologically. I have a hard time gauging how long or short ago a particular event happened.

[MB2] Within the last one or two months, sure, but beyond that, things get mixed up fairly easily.

[JS] Yes, but it is a struggle.

[JA] I can't tell you what I had for my meals this week in order, or what I did on exact days this week. I often will say, "Yesterday, this happened" but in reality it was a week ago.

[CS2] Sometimes. Only relative to bigger events – like this was before/after I got married or moved cities.

[AY] With some effort, yes.

*

Do other senses, such as smell and taste, trigger memories?

[JK2] Yes they do. I may not be able to recall a smell in my head, but encountering the smell in real life can absolutely trigger memories. Sawdust and flannel are associated with my father, lilacs with my mother, etc.

[SR] Yes. For example, the scent of vanilla has taken me to one happy place for a couple of decades now :)

[JR] Yes. Especially smell, but I think that's true of almost everyone. Hearing songs can definitely trigger memories – where I was when I first heard it or whose favourite song it is. I also remember song lyrics for decades. I can sing along with some songs after only hearing them once or twice. I even remember inflections during certain parts of the song and can mimic them. I'm a good mimic in general, and I'm relatively good at accents.

[JL] Yes, but rather as recognition device, not emotional connection.

[PW] Yes, although typically only for strong connections. My first memory is smell-related, and I still cannot eat a particular food because I associated it with a friend that got car-sick. I also often recall memories associated with specific sounds.

[RH] Yes. Cherry tobacco; the smell of it always reminds me of my father.

[MC] Yes. Smell and taste both remind me of past events.

[MB2] My mechanical senses (touch, hearing, proprioception) can definitely trigger memories (again, as concepts or facts, not images), but my chemical senses, smell and taste do not. For example, I can hear a song and remember hearing it live at a concert, or listening to it in the car with a friend.

[Anonymous] Yes, music, smell, and taste can all trigger memories. But again, in words. Because I also stored the music/smell/taste in words in my memory. E.g., I have certain music related to my previous relationship, I have the smell of Palo Santo which reminds me to spiritual ceremonies, etc.

[TM] I often have a very diminished sense of smell. When I can smell, it totally triggers memories. Same with taste. Sound really triggers memories for me.

[JT] Rarely. Songs are more likely to trigger memories (I think because music is very emotional for me).

[TS] I recognize smells and tastes and can often connect them to old concepts. I'm not sure if they trigger actual memories as often as they do for people without Aphantasia.

[L] No triggers here. My daughter told me that when she gets a whiff of the perfume that she wore in high school that tons of memories come flooding in! I have such a peaceful life! Ha!

[JS] Taste has no trigger.

[AY] Occasionally but it is extremely rare.

[ST] No.

Chapter 8: Living with the Condition [work and at home]

As has become clear in this book, Aphantasia can impact upon a number of different areas in Aphants' lives. In this section, Alan and his fellow contributors discuss the impact of Aphantasia on their work and home lives.

*

[Alan] Upon learning of my Aphantasia, I was able to realize and understand how frustration was brought on by me not being able to learn, or remember past events (both short- and long-term), or view my own historical mental imagery. These may not seem significant things in themselves, or individually, but the collective impact upon my confidence adversely affected me a lot. It meant I could not perform the tasks that others seemed to complete with ease.

I knew I could not complete work or tasks in the way others could; at the time I put the variations in ability down to intelligence, and a lack of it on my part. Even if I knew how to say how I felt, and the experiences I was having, I was unable to articulate my condition with words that others could have understood.

I left school at 16 and got a job working for a petrochemical company making models of oil refineries and oil rigs. It was brilliant because it meant I was making a model from a drawing – I didn't have to imagine what things looked like and I didn't need to have a vocabulary to explain or understand it.

Looking at my working history more broadly, I have spent 15 years in building concepts and ideas (innovation). My work has involved me thinking and imagining new concepts, alongside social and societal changes, which could affect the automotive market. Initially, I started the job thinking very simply about just a product, but as time has progressed, I have started to think differently. Over the years, I have developed coping strategies to assist me because of my Aphantasia, although this does mean I have masked the effects of the condition and it has taken time to strip back my behaviours to the actual thing that I'm concealing.

To assist me, and as mentioned, I take lots of pictures with my phone. This has become my digital memory. Before the age of smartphones and personal computers, I used to write lists for everything in an attempt to remember or recall the facts or information later. I use my iPhone as my list these days, recording things of importance. I would struggle without reminders on my phone and computer; my mind cannot remember all the things I need it to. Any additional help I can give it helps.

I think I follow unwritten rules that help me in everyday life. For tasks where people use stored images in their minds (for example, where they have put their phone/keys/etc.), I always put things in the same place in the house. I park my car in similar parking spots in carparks so that I have a general idea of where I left it should I not recall its exact location.

Emailing information to my own email address is a regular thing. I do this at least once a day, whether tweets, websites of interest, or simply pictures. I keep my emails and store my digital pictures in multiple locations.

I have travelled a lot for work, to America, Europe, and Asia. I always check the airport I am landing at, to see its layout before flying, looking at exits and taxi ranks. I plan the journey including printing off the hotel address. I never take a flight with stops (always direct flights); the thought of a complex flight involving stops would be too much.

How has Aphantasia affected your work life?

[AS] I'm not really sure it has. I lived so long without even knowing I had it. I guess maybe my career choices were affected? I was always interested in graphic design, but could never quite 'get there'. I just thought I didn't have a talent for it, but after finding out I have Aphantasia, I'm pretty sure that's the reason I had trouble in my design classes in college.

[RW] I'm a software engineer and I think it hurts me in some ways and helps me in others, but is a negative overall. I think a lot of explanations use visuals to drill information into you, and it doesn't help me learn. Also, not being able to picture layouts in my mind makes projects that have a web design aspect a pain in the butt. I think the way that Aphantasia "helped" is that it forced me to be good at grouping information in my head and reasoning things out verbally.

[LH] I worked in a primary school for many years and absolutely dreaded the thought of being asked to put up a display. It's one of my worst nightmares and haunts me even years later. It probably seems petty, but it's like asking me to perform major surgery on someone. I just don't have the right tools to do the job.

[MH] It's handicapped me for long-term prospects. Ambition is not present because of the inability to visualize plans and ideas and put them into action. Even small tasks require some type of visual acting out beforehand, and I suffer here as well.

[JT] Not noticeably. I mean, I didn't go to school for architecture or history, because I wouldn't be good at those. I went to school for nursing, which is conceptual and caring, which are things I am good at.

[ML] I work in a customer service role, and have to work to memorize names and faces. I can sometimes go months working with a person, and still struggle to remember their name. I try to relate them to a family member so that I can grab at the name that way. Faces – well, imagine! I tell everyone that I am face-blind.

[Anonymous] When I first found out about Aphantasia, I had some trouble convincing myself that I could keep doing the graphic design task I was in the middle of at the time. It took several weeks to get over the 'Oh my god, everyone else has this extra ability that seems like a magical power and I am severely disadvantaged because I don't have it' feeling. I had to repeat to myself that I had survived 28 years without it and done perfectly well, that my art/graphic design skills are serviceable if not top-5%, that I'm good at writing and 3D thinking, and many other things. I had trouble keeping on task for a while as I rethought my life (like when you get to the end of The Sixth Sense and you rethink what's happened in the film, but for your entire life), and then after that because I'm quite interested in the science etc. behind it; I don't think my boss(es) noticed. I don't tell people about Aphantasia in my professional life for fear they'll have a similar reaction to my own original reaction – how can this person do these tasks when they're lacking what everyone thinks is a fundamental thing?

I'm still not completely sure I understand how visualizing works, and I know I assume it can do more things than it actually does (for instance, one of my early questions was 'Why doesn't everyone have a photographic memory?'). I keep thinking of things that would be easier if I could visualize (memorizing/rehearsing presentations, looking at a conductor and seeing the sheet music in my head), but I have my own ways of doing this. I manage okay, and people have said visual memory sometimes doesn't help much anyway.

More generally, I've worked as a draughtsperson (3D thinking and drawing skills) and I'm currently completing a PhD in sociology (writing skills), both of which might be related to my Aphantasia, but it's probably a lot more complex than that.

[BM] As far as I know, my work life has not been significantly affected by not having a mind's eye. I am very good at abstract thinking, at finding patterns in data, and at testing alternative hypotheses for accounting for those patterns. I do not know whether or not this is related to not having conscious mental sensory experiences since I have many colleagues that are also good at it but have a mind's eye.

[AS2] Apart from not being able to recognize people, I don't think it has. I teach adults with learning difficulties and disabilities who often need their own memory triggers and things repeated constantly, and so I don't really have any issues with doing that.

[JR] I never thought about it, but it probably did. I was a librarian for 17 years at a liberal arts college. I'm not very organized – losing things in my work area was the norm. I am the worst file keeper. The worst.

Once I needed to write the copy for a library conference, which was easy but I couldn't imagine how the finished product would look. There was a reason that I needed to (can't remember now) but try as I might I couldn't imagine the final product. Probably why I'm a huge fan of templates for those kinds of projects. Most of my jobs required me being a good communicator, which I am. Besides being a librarian, I've been a counsellor, bookseller, proof-reader, editor. I've taught classes – keeping track of detailed paperwork was an arduous process for me.

I am not good at putting things back together even if I watched them being taken apart. Directions aren't always useful to me.

I am really good at writing procedures. Mine are so clear that rarely did people have to ask for clarification.

When I had to use equipment, especially when hooking things up and remembering what went in which socket – that was hard for me. I was at a total loss sometimes. I had to write it down if I wanted to get it right and even then...

[CS] I can't remember faces which I think may be part of Aphantasia. I work with children and adults teaching them to horse ride. It's really difficult especially with new clients to remember who they are. If they take their riding hat off, I am even worse as I'm so used to seeing everyone with hard hats on. The older clients I'm ok with, but if I see them away from my work, I would have real difficulty placing them, which makes me seem rude I think.

[MC] I am a graphic designer, and I think what gives me an aptitude for it is that I have a lot of practice organizing things visually. I need to organize things well outside of myself because I am not able to organize anything in my mind. However, I think this line of work would have been much harder before computer-aided design. I am able to save multiple versions or try things out in real time using a computer.

[VD] I think it inadvertently has guided me because my strengths were different, but I don't think it has directly affected my work.

[TM] Hmmm... I'm not sure. I'm a therapist and a school counsellor. My memory is great, so that helps me remember other people's stories. I was a special education teacher for 15 years. I think my early struggles with learning, perhaps Aphantasia-related, helped me to be a better teacher.

[Anonymous] Before I started travelling, I had a very good job as a strategy consultant in the aviation business. My strengths were being very analytical, detailed and logical, zero-defect, structure, etc. And my key development areas were visualizing concepts, improvisation, and slide design. Makes a lot of sense now that I know I have Aphantasia!

[JA] I struggle daily with organization and learning. I am really capable emotionally of connecting with people and animals, but for typical job strengths, I am terrible. I do not work well with limits and detailed rules and processes.

[JS] Not particularly as I work in a very factual, scientific profession.

[MU] I wanted to be a fiction writer and never did. Only now do I realize I did not pursue it because of my inability to visualize what I would write about. I am a writer (a poet, and a very good one), but my life would have been different, I am sure, if I had known how to work with myself and with this condition.

[RH] I am an extremely fast learner, and I make a lot of connections to things. I also tend to want to understand the big picture where others are often working in a very silo-ed way. Because I have so many interests, I am able to connect things that others can't. I can often put together solutions for business problems that others didn't see.

[MR2] It's made it difficult to switch jobs, especially to learn the names and faces of people I work with. It typically takes me about six months just to remember the people I work the most with.

[MR] I don't believe it did to a huge extent. I had one manager who had run a course I attended and who, a few weeks later, asked me a question about a mathematical equation he had covered. When I couldn't remember without going back to my notes, he demanded that I tell him exactly what he had covered from beginning to end. When I couldn't, I had to sit through the whole course again or lose pay for not meeting my objectives. I made more copious notes and memorized them and the order but wasn't asked again.

[KB] It hasn't affected it at all. I was the youngest manager in my corporate work and was well respected and got excellent reviews.

[L] When I didn't know I had it, it didn't affect me. Now when I look back, I see how I was not able in some ways, but I'm capable in others.

*

Here, contributors detail particular strategies and behaviours that help them to deal with Aphantasia.

[Anonymous] I've always taken a lot of notes in meetings etc., which help jog my memory pretty well later (I can then remember the situation, and more than just what is on the page).

[MB2] I do take a lot of notes and test my knowledge frequently on things I absolutely need to remember, like important dates in the future. Sometimes, I will repeat the speech of others in my head in order to remember it better.

[MC] Writing things down definitely helps. My mind feels like a void – often I can't leave anything detailed there (like a list or an address) and expect to come back to it intact, unless I am very familiar with it or work hard at it. I think the act of writing something down is also a tactile/spatial thing that helps solidify thoughts for me.

[TS] If I'm writing a story, I always make separate notes to remember how I initially described someone. Otherwise, I might well forget and then describe the person differently later in the story.

[AS2] I'm always jotting down notes for myself and emailing myself messages to remember.

[AY] I use both notes and verbal cues to help me remember things. If I place something somewhere, I will say out loud what I've done. I find it easier to remember saying something, than remembering an action.

[RH] It's funny, I take a lot of notes, but rarely refer to them. The act of writing the notes helps me to remember most of what I was writing. I typically only look back for a date, a specific name, or to ensure I remembered all the action items.

[BM] I don't "deal with" not having a mind's eye. It is just the way I am. I write things down at meetings more to help fasten them in my memory than to be able to read about them later. I like using a blackboard/wipeboard to help systematize data, work on analyses, and organize concepts for research articles and lectures. However, most of my colleagues have a mind's eye and they use the same methods I do.

[CS] I try to associate people with things to try and remember them, until I can actually remember them. I had one child that I had to remember by the glasses she wore; I'm glad she didn't change them. Also, I call everyone 'mate' or avoid using names where possible, in group lessons, so not to upset the clients whose names I can't remember. Some days I can forget people's names that I have known for years. I don't think it really affects me anywhere else really.

[GD] Notes… Lots and lots of notes. I also have no problem asking for things to be repeated.

[MH] I have sticky notes all over my desk and work, and I often write on my hands and arms. But then I have to force myself to take an extra step to remind me to read the notes whereas a normal person would simply remember they had written the note. I can't even visualize me looking at the note to read it in the first place.

[MR2] Yes, I take lots of notes, but it doesn't always help me to remember things. It helps to have Facebook to see current pictures of people, and a calendar app on my phone for important dates and appointments.

[VD] I think now that I have adapted to Aphantasia that it would reflect in how I do things, but it's hard for me to say how yet. When I take notes, it's a branching tree system usually (like Windows explored where you have subfolders) which I haven't really seen many people do for notes but it works for me.

[MU] I used to keep diaries for years – since elementary school. Just last year, I realized to my horror, that all of those diaries meant nothing. All the things I had written about were as though they had happened to someone else. I had no memory links to them.

[PW] I have over the years started getting almost compulsive about using electronic calendars and simple note apps to better remember things. I did not realize why when I started, but now [I feel] a lot of the need was due to Aphantasia and the difficulty of remembering event type things, even though I'm great at facts. I'm in the process of hopefully starting to make this an even bigger part of my routine, as I've been realizing it could really help with my communication hurdles.

[SR] I've always been a writer, and I like to draw (awfully, but...) to memorize important things.

[ST] To memorize holidays, I take pictures that string together to form a story.

*

How does your Aphantasia affect your relationship(s) with your family?

[LH] They still tell me things, and I have to say "Yes, I know what you mean, but I can't actually see it like you do." They can get a bit frustrated with me but I have to say I can't help that I can't remember this stuff.

[AS] It doesn't at all.

130

[AY] They don't really understand it or the complications it gives. I don't really talk to them about it at all though.

[RW] I don't think it does. I have a great relationship with pretty much all of my family, and they have been curious about this new discovery of mine.

[PW] I connect emotionally quite well with my wife, maybe even better than average, but I connect less so with my other family members. I do, at times, have communication shortcomings with my wife, but the more we both know about Aphantasia the less that is an issue.

I am very much a "doer" and less a "feeler", and while that is something my wife is very grateful for, it is also part of why connections are harder with my kids, as I end up making our relationship about what I need to do for them. Now that they are in college, and away from home, I tend not to think of them much.

I also don't feel connected very much to my parents or sisters, although I now know my mother also has Aphantasia, and maybe my sisters too. So, it's as much about their lack of connectedness as my own.

[KB] Apart from a few small miscommunications it has no impact on my relationships.

[BM] Not having a mind's eye does not affect my relationships with my family that I know of.

[CS] I think my relationship with my family has been affected, I know deep down that they weren't horrible to me, but I struggle to remember positive memories, and it's really difficult not to get upset. My brother and sister are a lot younger than I am so when they do nice things with my mum, it's hard to remember that she did those things with me too. I think that's why she made me memory photo albums. I try to remember that the issue is with me, but it's really difficult. Actually, I think it probably became easier when I discovered I had Aphantasia because then I had a reason not to remember these memories, and it was easier to believe people when they said they did nice things with me too. Then the memory books came along, and that helped too.

[DS] It doesn't affect it at all.

[TM] Mostly it has no impact at all. Occasionally it will cause frustration with my husband when I can't remember where kitchen items belong.

[ML] I think it makes me semi-detached. I do not miss people when they are not there. My children and grandchildren are dear to me, in a muffled way. I am fiercely protective of them but am not bothered if they don't visit or call. Basically, they get in touch when they need me or my help – the rest of the time they get on with their lives, and I get on with mine. But I think that leaves them feeling as if I don't love them at all. I do, but only when they are with me, when they go away they really cease to exist, except as a 'story'.

[MR] It has given them plenty to laugh about over the years and caused me endless frustration but, given that I am 64 and only discovered I have Aphantasia a year or so back, I think we have done very well.

[SC] I get along with everyone pretty well, but my job involves not seeing any family for long periods of time; I often go 3-4 months without hearing from them. I've never been homesick; I guess that's because I can't think of them easily.

[JA] I usually feel misunderstood and judged. I put a lot of effort into loving people, by listening, supporting, and being active at keeping in touch with them. However, when I need that same effort back, it does not happen.

I am honest with myself and am painfully aware of my shortcomings. However, most people do not sense themselves enough to examine their flaws truthfully, and they do not like them pointed out. My family tends to be critical, even mean, when feelings are hurt and will lash out with words in a cruel way. I readily accept and apologize for my negative actions... yet, if I even kindly but honestly criticize them – "I really love you but you are being unkind" – I get a verbal lashing. Being more emotionally aware is a blessing and a curse.

[JK2] It doesn't. Now that my husband knows about it, we tease each other in a good-natured way about our ability (or inability) to visualize.

[JK] I haven't really told them because it wouldn't change anything, I don't think it would matter.

[JL] Nothing serious really, although for most of my young life my father told me not to sit close to the TV, explaining that if he's unable to see something clearly, he uses his imagination to get a better image. I wasn't ever able to understand what he meant, but I was trying. We understood each other just last year, after he told me about this in the theatre and I confronted it with my version of imagination.

[JR] Not much. Though I think the fact that I misplace things may be related to Aphantasia, e.g., I don't remember where I put my keys, glasses, etc. several times a day because I can't 'see' where I last put them. My husband has to wait for me to find things (though he's good at finding them for me) and that can be frustrating for him. I'm frustrated with myself as well! Saying 'I'm putting my purse on the door handle,' helps because then I have a verbal clue. But I just recently started doing that.

[JS] I'm not able to visualize [family] faces at all, which I find quite sad. I think I've got a relatively normal relationship with my family. However, I do need to remember to keep in touch because I don't have daily contact with them and can forget.

[MB2] My relationship with my family is fine, though I live far away from them and have for over a year now. I find that it is easy to forget about them, feel disconnected and communicate much less if I don't see them very often, which I think is a product of Aphantasia. So the saying goes: out of sight, out of mind, out of reach.

[MB] It doesn't.

[MC] It saddens me that I can't revisit or relive good memories with my family, things like my wedding or vacations. I think that when I am alone, I am very much alone because I do not have visual memories to fall back on.

[MU] I explained about Aphantasia to them just last year, when I learned about it and my weaknesses. They are very kind and supportive.

[SR] My loved one visualizes in 3D, and his visualizations can move and turn and so on. He loves to woodwork and do all kinds of stuff with hands, and loves to talk about his plans, designs, and layouts with that huge inspiration glowing in his eyes... And there I am, trying to "see" it as hard as I can, and be amazed about the glorious idea – and it has always ended a bit lame.

When we didn't know about Aphantasia, I guess he (and me myself, too!) just thought I'm a bit slow to understand some things that actually were happening because I couldn't visualize. Others have just got used to me saying, "That sounds awesome, but I have to see it to understand fully." I did that even before I know about this condition.

*

Are you good at navigating?

[SB] Noooo, I'm so bad at this. Like REALLY bad. I have no sense of direction; [I can navigate] only when I have walked/driven the way many times.

[JK2] I get lost easily unless I am following step-by-step instructions, probably because I can't visualize a map.

[TM] Not by a map. I have a good gut instinct on where to go, but I'm useless with maps.

[JA] Not at all. I have zero sense of direction. I will walk into a store at the mall and have no idea what direction I came in from. I get lost without GPS.

[JT] No. I am horrible with maps and directions.

[VD] Quite the contrary, It is a well-established fact with my friends and family that I am not to be in charge of navigation, ever. Even in areas I am very familiar with, I get turned around easy and generally don't like driving to new places.

[MH] I have no sense of direction and the same route to work I have taken for the last 15+ years becomes alien to me the second I close my eyes and try to visualize it. Also, I always tend to forget where I park my car. This happens on a daily basis.

[ML] No sense of direction at all. If I enter a town that I know from a different direction, I have no idea how to get about. I don't remember being somewhere, so can't just drive back as some people can. It's not that I took no notice, I just can't keep any pictures of the places. I get lost in any hospital, sometimes for ages! I am good at map-reading though – that is logical and easy for me.

[AY] No. I am the last person you ever want to be navigating. I struggle to remember road names and addresses.

[DG] Sometimes very well, other times – hopeless. I don't know why.

[RH] I am great with a map as a navigator to a driver. I am horrible at navigating without a map or GPS. I have no sense of direction.

[Anonymous] I'm extremely good at directions and generally know where north is, though I have a tendency to trust myself too much and then get very lost when I'm wrong. I'm from the Southern Hemisphere, and I get my north-point mixed up somehow in the Northern Hemisphere, so I more often get lost there. I'll be really sure I'm going east, but I'm actually going west. I'm not sure how I figure out where north is – something to do with the sun maybe? It seems a little far-fetched that I'd use the magnetic pole.

[JS] Yes, but it's very spatially orientated. Like I go out of here, turn right, continue until I get to X… The idea that people can visualize a map is annoying.

[BM] Yes, if I have a map or have memorized a route as a schematic. Otherwise, I am terrible at remembering routes even if I have travelled them hundreds of times.

[JK] Yeah, my spatial awareness is not too shabby.

[JR] I have a good sense of direction. I prefer street names, not landmarks when given directions, e.g., turn left on Cupcake St vs. turn left when you come to the giant hot dog. I don't get lost in my hometown but realize that sometimes, when I'm in an unfamiliar area of town, I can't get my bearings because I don't have a point of reference and it all seems like a big mess that I can't sort out in my head.

[KB] Yes. I have an excellent sense of direction. I can easily find my way back to a place after I have driven there once.

[Anonymous] I am a very good navigator. But I don't remember the way like 'turn right at the church and then turn left after the bridge', but I remember the way like 'I have to take the 4th street to the left and then the 8th to the right'.

[PW] I am great at navigating, even almost always knowing which direction I am facing – it's almost like I have a map in my head, even though it is not an image! I do have a hard time getting past the rare frustrations that I do encounter though, and I can forget what I am doing if there are engaging conversations at the same time since I tend to be singly focused.

[SC] Yes, I'm VERY good at navigation. I grew up in the bush, and being able to find your way home was vital. I've trained navigation for the army before. I can look at a map for two minutes, and then find my way to anything on that map without needing to look at it again.

Chapter 9: Downsides

This book has already touched upon some of the perceived downsides that Alan and his fellow contributors have experienced with Aphantasia. This section revisits some previously highlighted disadvantages and problems associated with the condition, as well as providing newer insights.

*

[Alan] One aspect that is strange and difficult, for family and friends, is that I do not remember faces at all. In fact, I can barely remember any details for anyone, including my parents, brothers, their wives, and their children. I cannot see anyone's face in my mind, ever. But I do know who people are when I see them in real life; they are familiar, and known, and some form of recognition and reorganization takes place in my mind.

Not being able to visualize family or loved ones has really affected me as I have grown older; it has certainly had the most impact on my wellbeing, and makes me feel most sad. I feel particularly despondent when I think about the deaths of family and loved ones. I have memories of their lives, but just like the other times in my life, I have no real detail.

I can't begin to imagine how people dealt with Aphantasia years ago, before the advent of digital pictures and videos.

Aside from sadness, I also experience envy. I envy other people's ability to have instant recall for mentally stored images, and even for their ability to create new ones in their minds' eyes.

Of the remaining downsides, I miss the ability to create a mental history as I take pictures of important life events; it's the small stuff that seems to matter.

The thing about any "downside" is that you first need to have enough perspective to know the range and scope of any situation or condition, and then to know where you are in that range. If you start with the premise that not to have something is a negative then just having Aphantasia is a negative in itself.

Previously, I have asked other sufferers to explain how they feel about having Aphantasia, and I was slightly surprised at their responses. I had thought everyone would be relatively downbeat about the condition but was surprised to learn that many were happy and would not change how their minds work. Maybe I am the one who is different? Could it be the engineer in me trying to get answers or understanding?

*

What would you say are the downsides to Aphantasia?

[ML] It leaves me as an outsider. A viewer of life, not particularly a participant. I don't like holidays or sightseeing – what is the point? You go, you see things, you leave, and it is gone. Not a trace or a sensation remains. You've seen one tree, you've seen them all.

Another downside is that I cannot re-create my Mum. I saw her once, large as life in a dream, and woke with her image in my mind. It was lovely but left me wondering if I would like to do that a lot. If the barriers came down, I may drown in the build-up of 'missings' that lie behind that dam – 66 years of loss might well kill me in one go.

I am envious of people who can 'see', but I am also envious of people who can run fast or create music. It is a skill that I lack, but do not really need – yet! I have Bi-lateral Uveitis, and it could blind me one day. I fear that. What will it be like to be physically blind and mentally blind? Not nice. I can't remember what my own children look like. I can create a word picture, but that will not help me if my eyes go. Then I would *need* to see with my mind.

[DS] Not being able to visualize IS the downside. Any other downside caused by that is more of a personal issue. Some people let that depress them. Some people feel limited. I don't feel this way. Like I said, it's just a style of thinking, and my style is different than others.

[AR] I am unable to relive happy memories, which is sometimes difficult to cope with. I wish I was able to picture things.

[JA] For me, I think it has been harder to learn in traditional settings and ways. I feel isolated and overlooked often. I rarely feel people relate to me, even though it is easy for me to "put myself in their shoes." I am sure I'd be a better artist and photographer if I could visualize. I am happy for those who can visualize. I am not envious; I feel a loss, but then again, maybe I wouldn't be as kind and caring without having Aphantasia.

[JT] For me, the biggest difficulty is thinking my whole life has basically been traumatic, because these are the memories I am easiest able to remember. While I have had a considerable amount of trauma, I think it would feel less negative overall if I had more "neutral" memories thrown into the mix. However, simply realizing this has been helpful, and therapy has been going much better as we are working on ways of processing and coping that account for my inability to visualize. :)

I appreciate the alternative connections my mind has come up with to compensate for being unable to visualize. I would like to know what it's like to be able to visualize, but it also seems like it would be quite overwhelming.

[TM] I had to work a lot harder as a learner, which caused me to feel like I wasn't intelligent. That had a long-lasting impact on my emotional health, but when I finally figured out my own learning styles, I was mostly able to move beyond that. Navigating can be hard, so I have to be flexible and know that I'll mess up. I'm pretty unorganized, which I also blame on Aphantasia.

Sometimes I long to be able to visualize, just so I could see what it was like. I think that I'd be less afraid of stillness if I had visualization skills. As it is now, if there is no sound around me, and no ability to visualize, I basically just want to jump out of my skin.

[AK] I'm happy with who I am. It would be fun to have images in my mind that I could control!

[Anonymous] I identify a little with Blake Ross's description of not being very attached to people – but then I don't like that I identify with it. I am shy, but I like people, and I've been extremely upset when people close to me have died or been diagnosed with a life-threatening illness (that sounds defensive…).

I don't 'miss' people all that much when they're away (except in extreme situations like my moving to the other side of the world), but I really enjoy their company when they're there or when I talk to them, and if I forget to organize get-togethers I feel something's missing. I wonder if it's a little like 'out-of-sight, out-of-mind', given I can't picture them; but then again it might not be related to Aphantasia at all – maybe it's to do with the autistic spectrum (I don't think I'm very much on the spectrum, but some of my wider family are). I often feel a little guilty that I don't feel as attached to people as they seem to be to me (or is that just my perception?).

I also struggle to find strategies to get to sleep. It usually takes me between 20 minutes and an hour to get to sleep, because my brain is turning everything over and my inner voice keeps going. TV immediately before sleeping helps, books don't (I have a habit of reading until three in the morning, so a book doesn't mean 'sleep' to me), and I can't do anything like count sheep or imagine a sunset. Well, I sort of can spatially, but it takes concentration which means I don't get to sleep.

[AS2] Now that I know I have this condition, I would like to be able to change how my mind operates; in particular, to be able to conjure up a visual image in my mind when reading a book.

[AS] I think it limits my creativity a bit. I'm a creative person, but not visually. I have a really hard time grasping concepts sometimes, and I can't create things out of my mind. It's kind of hard to explain.

Another downside is that I can't replay big moments in my life. I can't see my husband's face when he first saw me in my wedding dress. I can't just close my eyes and picture my now three-year-old son as an infant. I have to rely solely on pictures and videos. And sometimes, that makes me a bit sad.

[TS] I deeply wish I could visualize normally. Everything beautiful is just gone after I turn my head away.

If I break up with someone, it's almost like she might as well not have existed since I can never really return to those memories.

[AY] I tend to live only in the 'now'. I don't care about the past or future much because they are not relevant to me. In some circumstances, I do get jealous. I can't really remember my loved ones, and I'd like to. I'm a musician, but I can't hear music in my head, so it's harder for me to be able to create or play music. No, I prefer it this way. It's quiet and peaceful, and I think having a "busy"/normal mind would be too distracting. I like the way I am.

[CH] I can't predict what a new recipe will taste like. My husband can put together cocktail ingredients and put the test together in his head before actually creating the new drink.

I am happy as I am.

[CS] I have an MSc degree, so science is a big part of who I am. I want nothing more than to understand what people see. It literally kills me. I have to ask questions all the time, but I never understand the answers. I cannot even begin to comprehend how people visualize. It is a constant source of frustration. I have to push it out of my mind some days, like other things that I can't get an answer to. I cannot cope some days with not understand me, it's frustrating.

I don't know if I would cope with visualizing since I never have. It would be foolish to change my normality like that. Although I would like to see what everyone else does, even for a short while, just to understand.

[MU] For me, a horribly terrible memory. I have a certain degree of face blindness, too. This is especially terrible in my private practice, as I work with new people all the time. I have no memory of who they are once they leave the room.

When I learned about Aphantasia, I fell into a horrible depression. I am fascinated by how people's minds work and often ask people what their inner experience is like and if they have a mind's eye.

I would do anything to be able to remember my life and to remember what my relatives looked and sounded like. Mostly, I would want to have memories of raising my two sons and to access what they were like, and sounded like, when they were little.

[PW] For me, the only real downside is that I do feel very different, and I sometimes have trouble in social settings and with some communication. I see others online reporting significant problems, but they seem to be as much related to memory or learning style as to Aphantasia, and my memory of facts is great, and my concept/pattern-based learning style has served me well with math and more.

I am happy to be me!

[RW] I paint as a hobby, and I have always been frustrated with my inability to paint without a reference. Seeing artists post these crazy abstract images has always made me feel bad about my skills as an artist. Little did I know that they have a cheat sheet. That's probably what I'm most bitter about: I feel like I would be a much better artist without Aphantasia. I really wish that I could form an image in my head and draw from there. Additionally, I feel like sometimes – when drawing without a reference – that I make huge mistakes with perspectives and ratios. I don't think this would be happening if I were able to form a mental image to draw from.

[SB] You can feel isolated and sometimes it sucks when you have no sense of direction or are really bad at remembering faces because, in certain situations, it is necessary.

Sometimes, I'm sad and envious because I'd really like to be able to see pictures with my mind. It feels like I'm missing out on something, and I didn't even know this for the majority of my life.

Sometimes, I want to change [my condition] because it must be amazing to see real images in your head! I know that it isn't possible to change but I'd be willing to do exercises to "learn" how to imagine pictures.

[VD] It's hard to connect to people sometimes if I am trying to describe something. I use a lot of comparative statements and have, over the years, learned that it is not a very effective way to explain things to a lot of people.

[CW] For me, none.

[JK2] I honestly can't say if I feel that there is a downside. I haven't experienced anything else with which to compare my experience. I know what other people say they experience, but I couldn't say if that's better or worse than my own.

It's possible that I experience emotional memories more strongly than other people, though. I find that crying just because I remember the sad parts of a film or book is a bit inconvenient. I think the strongest emotion I have is confusion; do people really see images or are they experiencing the same thing I do but just describing it differently?

I find it fascinating that my father experiences a full-immersion imagination. That would be cool, but I don't feel like I'm missing out on something. So I suppose I'm happy with who I am and how this has played out.

[JK] I'm jealous that they can see, but I'm comfortable being who I am. I'd like to be able to turn Aphantasia on and off like a toggle so I could fully experience both sides.

[JL] [A downside is] quality of life, but by not having a comparison point I can't say what are the real downsides. I'd be happy to have the possibility of visual imagination because very, very rarely, in certain conditions, I regain the ability to imagine visually. But it's so very rare I just vaguely grab the concept – and it's usually connected to extreme tiredness while being drunk so I don't really remember it (it has happened two or three times in the last several years). I'm not trying forcefully to recreate these conditions.

[JR] Misplacing things, which is basically not remembering where I put things. I wish I could see my mom's face or my son's face when he was a baby. All I remember are pictures that I can 'see' though not via visualizations. It's the 'seeing but not seeing' action that I think a lot of people with Aphantasia describe.

I'm a little too old and wise for envy. I believe I've been very successful and able to live a full life.

No, I'm comfortable with who I am. When I hear about people who have arguments with others in their heads, just thinking about doing that makes my head hurt.

[JS] I find it very hard to keep in contact with people who I don't have prolonged, daily contact with. Once they are gone for longer than a few days, it's almost like they don't exist and the emotional response goes with it.

I've lived this long without [visualization] and wouldn't know what to do if I could visualize. Although I am very curious about what I lack, and wouldn't mind being able to experience it.

[KB] None. I am happy with who I am.

[L] Aphantasia does not make me unhappy. Every person has to find happiness within themselves. Having vision would not "make" happiness.

[Anonymous] I would love to know what it's like to visualize stuff, but only as an addition to how my mind works now. I'm very happy in general with the way my mind works!

[MB2] I feel that I don't appreciate my experiences as much as others do. Sometimes, I will forgo doing something expensive because I know I won't really remember the experience in a month or two aside from the knowledge that I did it.

I also sometimes feel like my Aphantasia has made me relatively emotionally disconnected. Images are very tied to emotions, and if I can't see something, it's hard for me to care about it in the long-term.

A lack of images also makes it hard to focus on what people say sometimes, but this may be just a problem of a lack of focus.

[MB] It's just how I am. I wasn't very upset when my mum died. I think it's because I can't imagine her.

[MC] I am not envious, but I am also not super happy about my lack of visualization.

I think that if I were to gain visualization at this point in my life, it would be overwhelming. For me, that risk of being overwhelmed – unable to escape from images in my own mind – would make it a hard decision to change that about myself.

[MH] I am still trying to come to grips with the magnitude of this revelation. The odd thing is I remember when I was in my 20s a strange feeling hit me all of a sudden that stayed with me for quite some time and that was the idea that everybody else on the planet had a third eye and I had only two eyes. It's weird, but now I see how appropriate that feeling was. From the bottom of my heart, I knew I was missing something, but I didn't have any clue what it was.

[I would like to change how my mind operates] especially for the sake of my music career which hasn't budged even though I have a world class voice. My voice teacher once told me, when he realized I was having learning difficulties but not yet aware of my Aphantasia, that God rarely gives a singer all the tools for an opera career. Some have good voices but are poor musicians. Some are fabulous musicians but have a mediocre voice. Others have just a little bit of each. So I figured my lot was having a world-class singing voice but nothing else to accompany it. Now I realize how true that assessment was.

I would like to have the option of mentally 'seeing/smelling/tasting/hearing/feeling'. To have a switch to turn things on or off would be good.

[MR2] It makes it more difficult to remember things, especially happy memories that you'd like to relive. I wish I was more creative and could remember things better, especially names and faces.

[MR] On the whole I am happy being me – but there are moments when Aphantasia generates:

- Sadness that I can't recall the faces of people I have lost.

- Frustration that I cannot envisage how things would look with certain changes, or how to put things together.

- Anger when people tell me I am being difficult because I cannot recall events the way they do.

[RH] I am envious of people [and] how quickly they can think about things. They can compute everything so quickly. But I know that the way I think gives me some advantages, like connecting everything that people don't see as connected.

If I had a magic wand, I would be able to turn on visual memory and visual thinking any time I wanted, like a light switch. I could move in and out, effortlessly.

[SC] When I first found out about it, I had some strong emotions, but that is normal for someone who finds out about something big like that – like if you only got told you were adopted after you turned 18.

I'm happy with the way I am, all of my "problems" have major benefits.

[SR] This sounds weird, but I love colours and I wonder – would I become as "colour-hungry" at times if they were with me, in my head, all the time? And how would it feel to "see" loved ones? And the daydreaming. I love to draw, but it's quite hard when I really have no clue what things or certain people look like. […] I'm not sure I would be happier, though.

[SR] Not sure. Maybe mostly curious and frustrated to not fully understand what it means to visualize. I'm happy for those who 'see in their head'. I'm not happy being who I am, but that may be more the depression I've had a long time, and not so much Aphantasia.

[VD] Curious, not really jealous. Every experience a non-Aphantasiac remembers is different, but mine are different too, so it doesn't really make me feel jealous. I would like to experience it once, seeing a picture in my head, but don't feel let down that I won't.

Chapter 10: Upsides

In this final section, Alan and his fellow contributors discuss the upsides that they see from having Aphantasia.

*

[Alan] I try to be positive in life. With Aphantasia, I also try to be positive.

One important perceived upside to having the condition is "clarity of thought"; my mind is not cluttered with unwanted mental thoughts and ideas – only the things I need to consider at that moment. Daydreams are momentary and disappear when I re-focus on the subject at hand. When I talk or listen to others, I don't have additional images pop into my mind, distracting me. Perhaps my mental focus is clearer than most because images don't distract me?

I know from other people that bad memories can be troubling to live with; I do not have these memories so I am not affected by experiences I would rather forget.

Another upside to me having these conditions is my inquisitive mind. When I need to clear my mind to focus on a particular problem, I think I find it is easier because it's relatively empty to begin with! Just filled with black.

One final upside to the condition is the community of fellow Aphantasia sufferers that I am part of. I have joined Facebook groups for people with the condition, and they are an excellent way of asking questions, proposing thoughts, and sharing interesting ideas. The sense of camaraderie is great and people are more than willing to talk about and share their thoughts and ideas, and support each other.

[MH] Everything I do is like the first time… there is no 'accumulation'. So when I'm at the gym, the reps and sets never become tedious or overwhelming where I feel like I should take a break and rest.

Along that same line, long road trips are quite fun. There is no thinking that I've been on the road driving for 10 or 12 hours. My body might be a little stiff, but my mind never succumbs to that creeping intensity of "accumulation" that I mentioned earlier. Also, there are no distractions in my mind were something catastrophic to happen. If I should see a mangled body in a car wreck, that image would leave my mind the second I turned my head. And most important of all, if my loved ones were to die, it would not affect me nearly as it would someone without Aphantasia.

Also, since I'm engaged to be married, I should bring up what I know to be an absolute fact and that is I will never get tired of seeing my wife's face. This might sound funny (and it is) but it's the truth. I told my fiancé, her name is Marina, that there will most certainly be days when I'll be out shopping solo and I will completely forget that I'm married. I also joke that I'll forget what she looks like… that is, until the next time I see her.

[MR] Like anything else, you learn to work within your abilities. Aphantasia is not a tragedy, an illness or a great burden to carry. It is different, but nothing you can't work around. No worse than colour blindness, being left-handed, or a Collingwood supporter (sorry, Aussie joke).

[JK2] I always have the words to describe what I want to describe. It might take me a few moments to sift through the pile, and longer to arrange the words into the sentences that I want, but I have them. I also never have to relive an awful scent or sound. The actual sound of nails on chalkboard makes my whole body seize up, but I can talk about it all day without actually experiencing the full force of that sound (or smell, or visual) – unlike some people I know. I think it allows me to be more objective when discussing or analysing certain topics.

[MB] I don't have nightmares or flashbacks of bad things that happened. I don't miss people who have died very much (not sure that is good or bad). My wife says she is jealous, she has an overactive visual imagination which stresses her.

[JS] I've found that it's always easier to tell the truth as lies require remembering and imagination. I find it hard to even go along with little lies, and it annoys my friends that I can't go along with lies.

[Anonymous] Not being able to relive negative memories with all the senses attached to them makes it probably a lot easier to get over things and move on with your life. Also, if a specific event has positive and negative experiences attached to it, I can more easily just 'decide' to put more emphasis on the positive parts and let go of the negative parts. I also don't mind people telling gross stories while I'm eating because I don't visualize it anyway, ha ha.

[MB2] I am resilient and "get over" adverse events easily. Traumatic experiences are easier to move on from with Aphantasia, as I can't "relive" those events again. I think this has made me a relatively mentally stable person, despite the anxiety disorder.

Images are probably distracting, too. I'd hate to know how distracted I'd be if I had a very vivid imagination!

[AS] I have anxiety and OCD, so I would say that an upside to having Aphantasia is that I can't picture things. I dwell a lot on my mistakes, and I imagine if I could actually "see" them, I would obsess even more than I already do. And being able to relive my worst memories would probably cripple me in more ways than one. So, it is a sort of protection, I suppose. Eventually, my worst experiences fade enough so that I don't dwell on them. I don't accidentally "see" them if the memory, or whatever, is brought to my mind because I don't have a mind's eye.

[AY] I have PTSD and an anxiety disorder, but it doesn't really affect me unless I'm actively talking about it. I don't get flashbacks or intrusive thoughts often at all. And they'd be much, much worse if I had a normal imagination. I deal with trauma and stress really well because I can detach myself from them and it doesn't affect me. [I have a] high pain threshold because I cannot remember pain, only the fact that I had it.

[CS] I think it helps me let go of the past, I don't hold on to bad memories in an emotive sense. I know they happened, but they don't bother me. I don't relive things; I'm not tortured by things in the past. I think that makes me pretty easy going and relaxed. I don't really know if there are any other upsides, because again I don't know what is normal. People get annoyed because my brain works almost in overdrive, but I don't know if that is linked or not! It suits me fine that I think very quickly and retain and recall information fast.

[Anonymous] It's difficult to tell what's related and what's not, and what's just part of a larger whole. I've wondered a little if I'm less susceptible to stereotyping others because I don't 'see' people when I think about them (but I still know I stereotype people anyway).

I've never had any trouble writing from a male or a female perspective – but that might be because I'm female, and so reading both 'boy books' and 'girl books' is socially acceptable for me, so I've had more exposure to both genders as protagonists. Writing a character seems less about their gender and more about their personality.

For me, personally, I think that my strong spatial and inner voice modes of thinking (rather than visual) have helped me with directions and writing. Otherwise, it's fun to chat about, and I'll be interested to see how our understanding of

Aphantasia, and the mind in general, evolves. I have an interesting perspective on how the mind works, comparing myself to other people. It's also a little like one of Blake Ross's friends said – a 'reverse superpower', which is kind of cool to have.

[AR] I would say the downsides outweigh the upsides; however, Aphantasia does mean I don't have to relive bad memories. I also never seem to get nightmares, but that may not be related. It does also keep me living in the moment, and I don't live in the past.

[SC] The biggest upside to Aphantasia is that it makes it impossible for me to visualize!! Along with my normal job, I work for the emergency services, and I've spoken with my workmates about what they think the hardest part of the job is. They all said it is definitely reliving traumatic things they have seen. They say that after attending a very traumatic job – especially when there is a fatality – they go home and have trouble sleeping, sometimes for weeks. They say that when they try to sleep, they see that person's dead face, or that guy saying "please don't let me die, man, I have a family." I once had another medic tell me he wishes he couldn't visualize, so that he wasn't haunted by the people who have died in front of him. Every time I tell other medics about how I can't visualize, they always say that I am extremely lucky, and that they envy me.

It is for this reason that I am glad I can't visualize. When I go home, after having someone die in front of me, I go to bed, close my eyes, and see nothing but black for a minute. Then, I'm off in my dream world, enjoying the freedom of flight, watching the universe pass before me.

[AS2] I don't think there are any.

[CH] I think mental imagery could be distracting.

[GD] It's just another way of being human and I really don't see any major upsides either.

155

[DS] One thing I noticed is that I don't have the same disappointments when watching a movie that was originally taken from a book. For example, some friends did not like a couple of characters in Harry Potter or Lord of the Rings. They had pictured them very differently, and it felt jarring, to them, to see them in a different way. I never had any preconceived image of those characters.

[JC] I am frightened of spiders and cannot picture them.

[JL] Up to now, I can only think that I cannot have a distaste or be disgusted with someone describing something. I've noticed a lot of people have "instant imaginations", meaning if you suddenly tell them something repugnant – they are not able to stop the visualization in their minds and they go "eeew." The same goes for dark humour or really repugnant jokes.

[JR] I am very observant – I people watch a lot, I notice things going on 'in the background' in some settings. Like in a restaurant, I may notice people having a heated conversation even though they haven't raised their voices. I will often create backstories about people I see, (e.g., an older woman and a younger man sitting together in a coffee shop… I may imagine that they are mother and son and are getting together to make plans for her husband/his dad's birthday). When they laugh, I imagine what the joke may be about. Often my imaginings are 'way-out,' like the people are aliens, etc.

I 'connect the dots' and see potential/possibilities where others may not. I guess you'd call that having a vision (without visualizing). When I was 10, for example, I saw my mom talking to her friends in the kitchen but because of their actions/reactions, as well as things I'd heard or seen earlier, I figured out that my mom was having a baby before she said anything.

[JT] I'm very empathic and logical, which is an odd combination, and one usually overrides the other depending on

156

the situation. But I attribute the increased development of both of these characteristics to being unable to visualize, and finding other ways to compensate and view the world.

[KB] Now that I have practiced yoga and meditation for a number of years, it is very easy to have a completely empty mind.

[ML] I never 'miss' anything or anyone. I do not grieve deeply. I tend not to hold grudges or stay angry at someone. I can move location/home etc. without 'looking back' (you know, I always thought that was just a metaphor – and cannot believe that people can actually 'see' stuff when they 'look back'). My children left home and I shed not a single tear. I used to think that people were 'soppy' and putting it on when they cried at weddings or when sending 'Sonny off to college', etc. Now I know that they feel things that I will never feel, not at that level. I get a bit sad at stuff like that, but never upset. Sometimes being 'semi-detached' can be a blessing.

[MR2] Being able to quickly forget something that is really sad or difficult. Some people get "stuck" and can't move on. Once I get past the initial difficult period, I can remember the facts about what happened without feeling the emotions and reliving the pain.

[ND] I don't necessarily think there are any. Some people will say that we don't relive trauma, but I am very aware of traumatic events in my life even though I don't see them.

[PW] There seems to be two main types [of Aphants]: those that think in words instead of images, and those that think in concepts/patterns. I am the latter type, and that seems to lead to being better at math and logic and more abstract thinking, including software development. It also may be partly why I focus easily on one thing, which is very useful in those types of careers, and I think may make someone like me a really good partner also.

[RW] My husband has always marvelled at my resilience to negativity and trauma. I think Aphantasia makes it easier because I don't recall the visual memories of the bad events into my mind.

[SB] You learn to adapt to a different way of living because almost everyone functions a certain way (i.e., seeing images in your head) but you are kind of "special" or "different" and you have to find your own way of getting through your everyday life – mostly without help because Aphantasia is a condition that isn't really known about in society.

[MU] I don't think there are any. However, I am usually in an extreme state of 'mindfulness'. I seem to live 100% in the present. I guess that's a good thing. It makes me feel very disjointed, however. I always have the sense something is profoundly wrong with how my brain is working and it makes me very sad.

[TM] I think that my auditory skills are strengthened due to Aphantasia so that is an upside. I'm just me, really, so I don't know if that is upside or not.

[TS] I forget bad things easily. I don't get side-tracked by images in my head. Talking about yucky things doesn't bother me.

[VD] As a whole, I don't think it's better or worse to have Aphantasia, just different. Case by case, one may be better but as a whole its just two different ways.

[L] I live in the now. I cannot live in the past. I cannot dream of the future. I have had many very spiritual experiences before I even knew that I was different than most people. I have done things differently, and that is OK with me.

Thank You

Thank you for reading this book about Aphantasia.

I would like to express a huge gratitude to all the contributors to this book; their insights and explanations of how they live with Aphantasia has helped give me a different understanding into the condition; a condition which I am still trying to define and fully understand for myself.

There is no "one size fits all" approach with Aphantasia; we all have differences in the effects of the condition and its impact which, when combined, give us unique perspectives on how we see it and explain it to others. Aphants often do not feel to be disadvantaged in living with the condition, whilst others may never become aware they have it. We are just scratching the surface of understanding people's personal experiences as well as the science.

In the future, I hope that research into Aphantasia looks at how people learn and adapt as they grow up, giving clues about how individuals like me could be taught to learn when content is provided visually and needs to be retained.

For me, this book is shining a light on this subject. I hope it helps to make people more aware of the condition.

Alan

I've Got a Stat For You: My Life With Autism by Andrew Edwards

At the age of four, Andrew Edwards was diagnosed with autism. "Go home and watch Rain Man," the specialist told his mother. "In all probability your son will be institutionalised." Determined to prove the specialist wrong, Andrew's mother set out to give her son the best life possible.

I've got a Stat for You is an honest and compelling account of one young man's journey to manage his autism and achieve his goals. Raised in a single parent household and encountering bureaucracy, bullying, and a lack of understanding from many around him, Andrew emerged from a turbulent childhood to win a Welsh National Young Volunteer Award, give speeches on his condition, and secure his dream job as a statistician at Manchester United Television.

From Wrexham to Buckingham Palace, and incorporating stories of The Simpsons, sport, music, and strange smells – *I've got a Stat for You* is a powerful and inspirational tale that shows how determination, a positive outlook, and the will to succeed can overcome all odds!

"Andrew's ability to fight against the odds is an inspiration to many others." **BBC Wales Today**

"It is an interesting read and it makes one feel like you actually know the author and are part of his life." **Autismnow.com**

"Absolutely a "must read" for anyone who lives or works with an autistic person- or for anyone interested not just in autism, but in the complexities of human communicaton." **Michellesblog.co.uk**

Write From The Start: The Beginner's Guide to Writing Professional Non-Fiction by Caroline Foster

Do you want to become a writer? Would you like to earn money from writing? Do you know where to begin?

Help is at hand with *Write From The Start* – a practical must-read resource for newcomers to the world of non-fiction writing. It is a vast genre that encompasses books, newspaper and magazine articles, press releases, business copy, the web, blogging, and much more besides.

Jam-packed with great advice, the book is aimed at novice writers, hobbyist writers, or those considering a full-time writing career, and offers a comprehensive guide to help you plan, prepare, and professionally submit your non-fiction work. It is designed to get you up-and-running fast.

Write From The Start will teach you how to explore topic areas methodically, tailor content for different audiences, and create compelling copy. It will teach you which writing styles work best for specific publications, how to improve your chances of securing both commissioned and uncommissioned work, how to build a portfolio that gets results, and how to take that book idea all the way to publication.

Comprised of 16 chapters, there is information on conducting effective research, book submissions, writing for business, copyright and plagiarism pitfalls, formatting, professional support networks, contracts and agreements, the value of humour, ghostwriting, and much more…

The Savvy Traveller Survival Guide by Peter John

Travel is one of our favourite activities. From the hustle of bustle of the mega-cities to sleepy mountain towns to the tranquillity and isolation of tropical islands, we love to get out there and explore the world.

But globe-trotting also comes with its pitfalls. Wherever there are travellers, there are swindlers looking to relieve individuals of their money, possessions and sometimes even more. To avoid such troubles, and to get on with enjoyable and fulfilling trips, people need to get smart. This book shows you how.

The Savvy Traveller Survival Guide offers practical advice on avoiding the scams and hoaxes that can ruin any trip. From no-menu, rigged betting, and scenic taxi tour scams to rental damage, baksheesh, and credit card deceits – this book details scam hotspots, how the scams play out and what you can do to prevent them. *The Savvy Traveller Survival Guide* will help you develop an awareness and vigilance for high-risk people, activities, and environments.

Forewarned is forearmed!

"If you desire to achieve something more, read this book"
Terry Byrne,
Chairman, Round World Entertainment

YOU WILL THRIVE
THE LIFE-AFFIRMING WAY TO WORK AND BECOME WHAT YOU REALLY DESIRE
JAG SHOKER

You Will Thrive: The Life-Affirming Way to Work and Become What You Really Desire
by Jag Shoker

Have you lost your spark or the passion for what you do? Is your heart no longer in your work or (like so many people) are you simply disillusioned by the frantic race to get ahead in life? Your sense of unease may be getting harder to ignore, and comes from the growing urge to step off the treadmill and pursue a more thrilling *and* meaningful direction in life.

You Will Thrive addresses the subject of modern disillusionment. It is essential reading for people looking to make the most of their talents and be something more in life. Something that matters. Something that makes a difference in the world.

Through six empowering steps, it reveals 'the Way' to boldly follow your heart as it leads you to the perfect opportunities you seek. Through every step, it urges you to put a compelling thought to the test:

You possess the power within you to attract the right people, opportunities, and circumstances that you need to become what you desire.

As you'll discover, if you find the *faith* to act on this power and do the Work required to realise your dream, a testing yet life-affirming path will unfold before you as life *orchestrates* the Way to make it all happen.

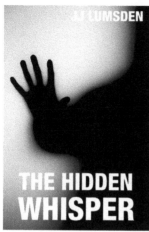

The Hidden Whisper by JJ Lumsden [parapsychology book series]

A paranormal puzzle smoulders in the desert heat of southern Arizona. At the home of Jack and Chloe Monroe, a written message "Leave Now" appears then disappears, a candle in an empty room mysteriously lights itself, and – most enigmatically – an unidentifiable ethereal whisper begins to permeate the house. What was once simply strange now feels sinister. What once seemed a curiosity now seems terrifying.

Dr. Luke Jackson, a British Parapsychologist visiting family nearby, is asked to investigate and quickly finds himself drawn deeper into the series of unexplained events. Time is against him. He has just one week to understand and resolve the poltergeist case before he must depart Arizona.

The Hidden Whisper is the acclaimed paranormal thriller, written by real-life parapsychologist Dr. JJ Lumsden, which offers a rare opportunity to enter the intriguing world of parapsychology through the eyes of Luke Jackson. The fictional narrative is combined with extensive endnotes and references that cover Extra Sensory Perception, Psychokinesis, Haunts, Poltergeists, Out of Body Experiences, and more. If you thought parapsychology was like Ghostbusters – think again…

This book works on many levels, an excellent introduction to the concepts current in the field of parapsychology… at best you may learn something new, and at worst you'll have read a witty and well-written paranormal detective story **Parascience**

An extremely well-written and suspenseful page-turner from real life parapsychologist JJ Lumsden **Yoga Magazine**

…a ghost investigation novel that has all the elements of a good detective mystery and spooky thriller…an engrossing haunting tale… an informative overview of the current theories on the phenomena. **About.com**

See all our books at

www.BennionKearny.com

Lightning Source UK Ltd.
Milton Keynes UK
UKHW021548210420
362053UK00018B/1963

9 781911 121428